ENDORSEMENTS

It's been said that "Discipline is the bridge between goals and accomplishments." The reason we often fail to see personal renewal or national revival is that modern Christianity neglects to bridge the gap between passion and action with biblical discipline. In this book, Parker Green exposes the reality that we can no longer rely on good intentions. It's time for action, and this book serves as your own personal trainer. I can confidently say that this book is a game-changer for anyone seeking to deepen their walk with Christ by developing transformational spiritual disciplines. This is the discipleship book you've been waiting for!

ALAN DIDIO
Host of *Encounter Today*

When I was a young man pursuing following Jesus, I read William Law's book, *A Serious Call to a Devout and Holy Life*. It changed my life! Parker Green has written such a book that calls his generation to take their faith seriously. With heartfelt transparency, biblical integrity, and practical applications, Parker has crafted a marvelous book. It moved me, and I believe it will move you…closer to Jesus.

ED PIOREK
Author of *The Father Loves You*

This book gets a huge "WOW" from me! Parker Green speaks the heart of the Father as he calls us all to a deeper and greater devotion to Jesus. God loves this book!

TODD SMITH
Lead Pastor, Christ Fellowship Church
Dawsonville, Georgia
Host Pastor, North Georgia Revival

WAY
OF THE
VICTORIOUS

THE ANCIENT POWER OF
SPIRITUAL DISCIPLINES

PARKER GREEN

DESTINY IMAGE® PUBLISHERS, INC.

PO Box 310, Shippensburg, PA 17257-0310

*"Publishing cutting-edge prophetic resources
to supernaturally empower the body of Christ"*

This book and all other Destiny Image and Destiny Image Fiction books are available at Christian bookstores and distributors worldwide.

For more information on foreign distributors, call 717-532-3040.

Reach us on the Internet: www.destinyimage.com.

ISBN 13 TP: 978-0-7684-6395-8
ISBN 13 eBook: 978-0-7684-6396-5
ISBN 13 HC: 978-0-7684-6473-3
ISBN 13 LP: 978-0-7684-6472-6

For Worldwide Distribution, Printed in the USA
1 2 3 4 5 6 7 8 / 27 26 25 24 23

CONTENTS

FOREWORD

We live in a charismatic generation that values experience over the centrality of God's Word. The call to pick up our cross and follow Jesus is not very appealing when we can run from revival service to another prophetic conference just to hear what our itching ears want to hear. In the midst of this crisis and deception, God is raising up voices like Parker Green to call us back to the place of discipleship that leads to simple and pure-hearted devotion to Jesus (2 Corinthians 11:3). It is such an urgent and necessary call in this late hour.

On my personal journey navigating through my love for revival and awakening, I have made three primary realities the basis for my Christian experience. I share them with you now as the reader in hopes that you might consider them in the days ahead.

1. The Church is a culture of truth, not a culture of feelings.

Timothy understood the dangers of building based off of our feelings and not the truth when he wrote and described the church: *"the household of God, which is the church of the living God, the pillar and support of the truth"* (1 Timothy 3:15 NASB). John Piper describes his thoughts so eloquently on the challenge this generation is having concerning our feelings and the truth when he writes and says:

> My feelings are not God. God is God. My feelings do not define truth. God's Word defines truth. My feelings are echoes and responses to what my mind perceives. And sometimes—many times—my feelings are out of sync with the truth. When that happens—and it happens every day in some measure—I try not to bend the truth to justify my imperfect feelings, but rather, I plead with God: Purify my perceptions of your truth and transform my feelings so that they are in sync with the truth.[1]

It's important that Christians understand that the way Jesus' words make us feel emotionally is not a good gauge of truth (see Matthew 19:22-25). When we hear the Word of God taught and preached, our first question should be "Is this true?" not "How did it make me feel?"

2. *You cannot separate Jesus from what He says and still have the real Jesus.*

Many in this generation are falling in love with a god of their imagination, not the God of the Bible. They enjoy separating the person of Jesus from the words of Jesus, and this is error. Mark 8:38 (NASB) says, *"For whoever is ashamed* *of Me **and My words**…the Son of Man will also be ashamed of him.*" In John 12:48 (NASB95) Jesus again says, *"He who rejects Me **and does not receive My sayings**, has one who judges him; the word I spoke is what will judge him at the last day.*" In Luke 6:46 (NASB) Jesus makes it plain concerning this issue when He asks, *"Why do you call Me, 'Lord, Lord,' and do not do what I say?"*

3. At the heart of discipleship is having our lives formed by God's Word.

In John 8:30-47, we clearly see that the crowds had a lot of admiration and even affection for Jesus. They "believed in Him" as the Messiah, but they were not prepared to yield to the requirements of true faith and to be changed to the core by His words. How we relate to Jesus' words determines whether we are His disciples or not. Jesus' words cut across our own desires, ideas, and lifestyles. The test of discipleship is whether we will bow to His truth or hold on to our own thoughts and feelings. Jesus never sacrificed truth for winsomeness. Seven times Jesus mentioned "truth" in John 8:30-47. When winsomeness becomes our highest priority, the truth always gets thrown under the bus. God and the devil are both asking the global church the same questions today: How much will it take for you to sell the truth? The approval of culture? Tax exempt status? Persecution? Proverbs 23:23 (NIV) says, *"Buy the truth and do not sell it."*

I encourage you to read this book slowly and consider what Parker Green has written. It's practical, sobering, and should challenge us all to repent and ask God to take us deeper in him. I have observed Parker's lifestyle, marriage, and family and can attest that what this man of God has written, he lives! And may that be said of each one of us—that we do not simply practice what we preach but rather we preach what we already practice. Jesus is truly worthy of all our affections and decisions.

JEREMIAH JOHNSON
Bestselling Author
Founder of The Ark Fellowship,
Altar Global, and Altar School

Note

1 John Piper, *Finally Alive: What Happens When We Are Born Again?* (Christian Focus, 2009).

INTRODUCTION

You are going to make mistakes. You are going to do this imperfectly, but we will aim for perfection. When it comes to so many things in our life that we want to do—what we dream about, hope for, and simply must get done—we get stalled. Why? Because so many people believe that they have to start something once they have all their ducks in a row, the timing is right, or when it's simply convenient.

When it comes to pursuing the path of spiritual disciplines, I often find this is the case with those I disciple and teach. They want to fast but a vacation is coming up. They want to be in the word more but their kids wake up early. They want to pray more but they don't know where to start.

The key, and it's a relief, is that it is far simpler than that. Either you are doing it or you are not.

Too many people frame their opinion of themselves or their accomplishments on their intentions. In reality, the only measurable thing in your life is the action you take and what that action produces in you and the lives around you that you influence. Not your hopes, your desires, your dreams, or your intentions. It's what you do that is actually measured in the end.

I want to encourage you to start no matter where you are when it comes to your faith. In order to be a master, you must constantly be willing to look like a fool. The point of this book is not to give you tips on how to improve your life, be a better Christian, or even be some kind of spiritual disciplines guru. It is to lead you to Jesus and help you develop tangible habits in your life that will create an anchor for you to continue following Him no matter what storms come your way.

Tools for The Path

At the end of each chapter are short activities to help you along the way. These are not laws and they won't solve every problem. Think of these as guideposts and steps to help you engage with following Jesus and staying on the path. Start when you don't know how. It's the only way forward and truly the only way to learn.

I pray that as you read and, most importantly, do what is written in these pages you draw closer to Christ than you have ever been before, and you become the type of person who is obedient to Him in all circumstances. God bless you and enjoy.

Chapter 1

THE PATH

Enter by the narrow gate. For the gate is wide and the way is easy that leads to destruction, and those who enter by it are many. For the gate is narrow and the way is hard that leads to life, and those who find it are few.
—MATTHEW 7:13-14 ESV

You Are Going Somewhere

My first time in the Sierra Nevada in California was in October and on my own in an '87 Honda Accord with 275,000 miles clocked on the odometer. I needed to get away. I was not an avid hiker, and I didn't really know what I was getting myself into. I just drove up and up and up until I came to the end of a mountain road in Kings Canyon National Park. There was no gate and there were no park rangers, so I found a campsite that seemed suitable (there wasn't another living soul there so I got the pick of the litter). I settled in with my cheap Coleman tent, an ax, a knife, and some cans of chili and a pound of beef for three days of retreat. On a misty morning I grabbed my backpack I had picked up at an army/navy store on the six-hour drive up, and I just started walking.

In reality, I was broken. I didn't know I was broken; I just knew I needed something different, something quiet and "away." I found what looked to be a trailhead and pointed to a spot on the map that seemed to be the place, Eagle Lake.

In the lower river valleys at that time of year the colors are extraordinary. The first few miles of the hike curved along a river surrounded by vibrant fall colors, and as far as I could tell I was the only one taking in the view. Luckily, the trail was well marked for a novice like myself. The hike climbed and switched back over a few thousand vertical feet. The last part of the trail was what looked like a wall of granite with nothing marking the trail but piles of stones left by hikers who had gone before. I was out of breath coming from sea level to almost 11,000 feet, but I was in love with this place. I finally finished this hike, which took more than half the day on this occasion.

I did not know why I was climbing or the particular reason I had come. It was simply a longing, so I went with it.

When I finally came to the top of the trail, I saw a lake surrounded by sheer granite cliffs dusted with the first snows of an early mountain winter. Then I knew. I knew why I was there. It was so quiet my ears started to ring. I tried to slow my breath only because I felt like my Clydesdale snorting was ruining the peace of that place. It was there and then that my path really began. God spoke to me, not so much in words or even in clear direction; He simply showed me I had come to the right place and to keep going. To keep climbing. To keep searching out silence so that I could hear. Away from the noise and the clutter of even my own mind. I could feel who I truly was, in all my brokenness, bubble to the surface when I shut out the world and found what the Irish call a "thin place." It seemed as if heaven had passed through a door and Jesus was taking counsel with me—had even been waiting for me in this place. My heart leapt for joy at the meeting; I knew I needed mending. To this day, I have not looked back. Through trial and error, through pain and grit, through victory and too many failures to count, I know how to get back on the path.

Since then, I have taken that silence with me everywhere I go. The silence amidst the noise where God can be heard, where I can give Him my full attention.

I want to show you how to do this. How to be with Him. Jesus says He is the way, and truly, Jesus Himself is the path. Something I have consistently said to the men I disciple is, "Jesus is the wilderness; we are the trail guides." Nobody comes to see the trail guide; they come to find Jesus, and if we can find the path, we can show others the way.

The world and, sadly, the church fall into the same trap. Looking for a path, looking for a way, looking for a destiny and identity, but trying to find it in themselves. This is the great fallacy of our generation, which has been aided by the church itself in many cases. A self-focused and self-soothing therapeutic deism isn't Christianity or discipleship at all. It's an aimless search to "find ourselves" when in reality we can find nothing until we find the true path, Jesus Himself. No identity, no purpose, no grand vision, and no trendy personality test (I'm looking at you Enneagram) can save your soul or tell you who you are. In fact, you can gain the whole world and lose the only thing of any real value.

Finding Yourself Really Means Finding Jesus

This is not a book about how to find yourself or a new, trendy discipline challenge. Any principles laid out here are in pursuit of the only true path, and that is Jesus. This is a book about Jesus and obsession with Him. This is the only real way to find the will and the tenacity to endure.

I do not practice spiritual disciplines in order to prove something or be a new Christian guru, but because He saved me. I want to know the Man who saved me—the God who saved me.

It is only when you realize who has actually done the saving that you can approach spiritual disciplines in the correct manner. If your angle is that you chose Jesus and you chose this path and you found the way, you've got it all wrong. He chose you, He saved you, He died for you, and there is no way around the fact that without Him you were a hopeless sinner with no solutions and nothing but judgment in your present and future. When you are pulled from a burning ship, you don't tell the captain of the coast guard frigate that picked you up that you found his ship in a vast sea all on your own. You say thank you and take the care given you. Then, if rightly inspired by your rescue, you join the coast guard, listen to the captain, and find those who were as helpless as you were on the burning wreckage of your life.

Discipline comes from passion and passion from discipline. Passion, the very word used to describe the day of Jesus' death, shows us the way. It is a way of dying so that you can truly live. The way of dying, the way of the cross—this is the path.

I understand that much of this sounds like extreme language, especially to pampered ears in the West, where persecution and even social pressure have been light. Where for the most part the church has catered to you instead of you being trained and disciplined in the way of Jesus. I understand—I have both been the seller of these goods and the purchaser; but biblical language is all I am relaying.

There is no partially following Christ. There is no middle ground. The church (that's us, not some institution to blame by the way) has ceded the field of battle to the desires of this world and the flesh, and we have all helped it along with our attendance, time, and financial capital. This is all of our fault, and it is individually our problem to solve. Nobody can choose this path for you. Nobody is going to answer to Jesus on your behalf on the day of judgment. You and only you will stand before Him, and all your choices and, more dreadfully, your deepest motivations will be laid bare before Him.

Of course, there is natural human interest, a provoking of the Holy Spirit to draw even nearer to Christ. This is an eternal path as we know, Christ is infinite. What I am speaking of is not this "onward and upward" call toward Christ. We will assume for the rest of this book that that is a given. What I am talking about is our general lack of obedience. The New Testament has over 1,050 commands to follow for Christians. At first this seems overwhelming, if Jesus had not so brilliantly boiled all the law and the prophets down to a single and symbiotic command:

> *You shall love the Lord your God with all your heart and with all your soul and with all your mind. This is the great and first commandment. And a second is like it: You shall love your neighbor as yourself. On these two commandments depend all the Law and the Prophets* (Matthew 22:37-40 ESV).

All the law and the prophets depend on this passage originally stated in the law in Deuteronomy.

The problem we run into with this passage is that we see the full hearted, from our deepest guts, holistic nature of this command itself. These words from the mouth of Jesus will radically transform a person's life and actions. What we see, unfortunately, in far too many cases is a lackluster attempt at some of our favorite scriptures and a twisting of even those passages in order to make caveats for our own weaknesses.

Of course, you will not be perfect. Yes, you will veer off course. We all have this tendency to become lazy and apathetic toward our walk and presumptuous toward God.

Practicing spiritual disciplines will not just give you a bunch of new habits that are trendy and fun to share with friends for two months. They instill a sense in us that following Jesus *and doing what He commands* is actually a possibility. Practicing what I write on these pages will by God's grace make you the *type of person* who is obedient to Jesus. So that you can open your map, the Bible, and this book and others like it, along with wise counsel, and get back on the path toward Christ.

Holy Dissatisfaction

I remember my deep frustration in trying to do what the Bible says and a deep dissatisfaction with the lack of power and fruit in my ministry. I eventually came to the incorrect conclusion that the words I was reading in the New Testament were an ideal—that they were true, but practically unattainable. I'm a competitive person, so playing a game I could not win led me to resignation and a heavy leaning on what I would now call "cheap grace." God would smooth out the edges and I would be fine in the end. I'll just keep plodding along and do whatever seems best.

What I did not know is that this resignation would simply lead me to a deeper dissatisfaction and frustration with myself, my faith, and then a projected frustration to those around me. Maybe this is you. Maybe you're indignant, flying off the handle at the trivial in yourself and others, railing at the church, pointing the finger at your pastors or fallen celebrity influencers (the favorite piñata of our time). If this is you, I have excellent news for you that took me years to discover, and I am going to give you that good news right now: the problem isn't any of those things—it's you.

Nobody can follow Jesus for you. Nobody can choose the path you follow in your stead.

Let's read a little story about money and personal responsibility that is deeply offensive to our modern society. As you read this, underline or highlight the portions that denote personal responsibility and individual accountability.

> For it will be like a man going on a journey, who called his servants and entrusted to them his property. To one he gave five talents, to another two, to another one, to each according to his ability. Then he went away. He who had received the five talents went at once and traded with them, and he made five talents more. So also he who had the two talents made two talents more. But he who had received the one talent went and dug in the ground and hid his master's money. Now after a long time the master of those servants came and settled accounts with them. And he who had

received the five talents came forward, bringing five talents more, saying, "Master, you delivered to me five talents; here, I have made five talents more." His master said to him, "Well done, good and faithful servant. You have been faithful over a little; I will set you over much. Enter into the joy of your master." And he also who had the two talents came forward, saying, "Master, you delivered to me two talents; here, I have made two talents more." His master said to him, "Well done, good and faithful servant. You have been faithful over a little; I will set you over much. Enter into the joy of your master." He also who had received the one talent came forward, saying, "Master, I knew you to be a hard man, reaping where you did not sow, and gathering where you scattered no seed, so I was afraid, and I went and hid your talent in the ground. Here, you have what is yours." But his master answered him, "You wicked and slothful servant! You knew that I reap where I have not sown and gather where I scattered no seed? Then you ought to have invested my money with the bankers, and at my coming I should have received what was my own with interest. So take the talent from him and give it to him who has the ten talents. For to everyone who has will more be given, and he will have an abundance. But from the one who has not, even what he has will be taken away. And cast the worthless servant

into the outer darkness. In that place there will
be weeping and gnashing of teeth" (Matthew
25:14-30 ESV).

We have in this parable not a few harsh realities. The context here is Jesus teaching on what the Kingdom of Heaven is like. We, as sons and daughters of God, are stewards of that Kingdom until He returns, and we will give *a personal account* of what we have done with the gifts He's given us. The pinnacle of the story, and the twist at the end that Jesus often throws in, is the judgment of the man with one talent. Even more, the judgment of the man who was given ten talents. These two judgments contrast not in what was given at the outset, but in how they thought of their master and whose responsibility it was to steward what had been given.

The man who was given "less" (which, by the way, was a *gift*—it was not owed to him) saw the master as a cruel and harsh man who took from work that was not his. The man with ten talents understood the gift and the corresponding responsibility and weight that came with being given such a task by his master. In this story the master does mete out an unfair judgment. Although the hearers would have been offended, everyone who reads this is mostly offended because they understand the judgment to be righteous and there is no way to logically circumvent it.

Those who were deeply loyal to the master and knew him to be a righteous, holy, and loving master did well with what they were given. He who spurned the gift and misjudged the character of the master was severely judged.

What we wrestle with here is the concept of kingship and ownership. Our conclusion is the same as those in the story: "Really? You're going to give the rich guy ten cities and then even more wealth?" A talent would have represented about one full year of labor. So from our perspective, the man who buried what he had and gave it back to the master should have at least continued to be a servant, he just needed some gentle correction. The wise and faithful steward, who multiplied his ten talents, what does he get more for? Unfortunately for many of us, we start from the wrong perspective altogether.

The master owns everything, including his servants' very lives. The very fact that they are given the talents in the first place shows a level of trust from the master to rightly deal with *his property*. This is the perspective we need to start with. The second is not just a matter of money, but of responsibility. The talent was a "weight" or "unit of measure" of responsibility given to these three men to do business with. The man with ten talents was given even more because his actions up to this point had shown the master that he was faithful (multiplication) and responsible. Any astute boss, king, or leader of any kind knows that if you want something done you give it to a busy man. The cities and the extra talent were going to be taken care of well. It would, in fact, be unjust to the entire kingdom and especially to those who inhabited the cities to give them to someone who had shown no promise and could not carry the weight of responsibility.

At the outset of your life in Christ, you have been given a gift. This is everything that falls under your sphere of influence and responsibility. You are commanded, by the word of the King, to multiply what has been given to you. In this Kingdom, begrudging maintenance is not faithfulness—multiplication is. Your very life now belongs to the King, and indeed it did from the beginning. You were set free by Him, with the purchasing price of the cross, from your besetting sin and self-destructive and self-centered patterns of living that only lead to death.

So your King gives you life. If seen correctly, life is responsibility properly shouldered in loving service to Jesus who *set you free*. Every breath, thought, word, and action now counts toward something, and you'll be judged based on these actions.

This is the path laid out before you: to take captive every thought, discipline your body (flesh) and make it your slave, and renew your mind according to the word and not the world.

Some at this point will scream, "*Grace! Grace! What about grace?*" What is it that you think grace truly is? Can't we just live by our feelings? Paul the apostle makes it clear:

> *What shall we say then? Are we to continue in sin that grace may abound? By no means! How can we who died to sin still live in it?* (Romans 6:1-2 ESV)

May it never be. Shall we use our freedom as license to stay like a spoiled child in our faith? Again, take a look at the letter to the Galatians.

For you were called to freedom, brothers. Only do not use your freedom as an opportunity for the flesh, but through love serve one another. For the whole law is fulfilled in one word: "You shall love your neighbor as yourself" (Galatians 5:13-14 ESV).

Should we ignore that passion so deeply stirred in us by our very life being saved and set in eternity with Christ?

And it is God who establishes us with you in Christ, and has anointed us, and who has also put his seal on us and given us his Spirit in our hearts as a guarantee (2 Corinthians 1:21-22 ESV).

Should we hold grace lightly and treat the mercy of God's love with disdain and sloth?

Since then we have a great high priest who has passed through the heavens, Jesus, the Son of God, let us hold fast our confession. For we do not have a high priest who is unable to sympathize with our weaknesses, but one who in every respect has been tempted as we are, yet without sin. Let us then with confidence draw near to the throne of grace, that we may receive mercy and find grace to help in time of need (Hebrews 4:14-16 ESV).

Of course not.

Grace is a gift to keep us on the path. We must be faithful with it. It is not some cosmic get out of jail free card to let us continue life as usual. Yes, grace is a free gift—it couldn't be any other way. You were on your way to hell, and you were saved and are being saved by Jesus Himself as you continue to look upon Him and be transformed from glory to glory into His image.

Grace is not a free ticket. Empowering grace is a responsibility and a gift at the same time, as kingly gifts so often are.

So what is it that will keep you on the path in the midst of trial, stupidity, wealth, success, poverty, and disappointment? What keeps you on track no matter what?

Here is what I like to do, and I think this will help you. Write down your story, spare no gory detail, of how you were saved. Remember and keep in your memory as your north star the saving work of Jesus in your life and how everything changed. Get back to the fundamental truth that you had no hope in the world without Christ, and let it recalibrate your heart and your attention on Him. Remember that you are truly and deeply loved on a scale you cannot imagine. Then, in turn, you can begin to take the path of the great commandment laid out earlier in this chapter.

Stay on the path, and keep staying on it.

Chapter 2

THE CHOICE

To another he said, "Follow me." But he said, "Lord, let me first go and bury my father." And Jesus said to him, "Leave the dead to bury their own dead. But as for you, go and proclaim the kingdom of God."
—LUKE 9:59-60 ESV

As I am writing this, the only software platform currently available to me to write this book is "notes" on a ten-year-old MacBook on a flight where the Wi-Fi isn't working, sandwiched between my wife and another passenger.

I made a commitment to myself that today I would write. So I here I am.

We all make internal commitments. To lose weight is the most infamous; but it could be one of a hundred other hopes, dreams, relationship commitments, basic tasks, time in the word and prayer—on and on they go. Promises that we make to ourselves. Too many of them are broken, and broken often.

Why do some keep these promises, it seems, far easier than others? Why do some men and women become giants of the Christian faith? No, I do not just mean famous preachers and worship leaders, past or present. What I mean is people who consistently seem to overcome difficulty and suffering and the weight of great responsibility in their lives while they *continue* to grow in their faith and substance as a disciple of Jesus.

I believe it is because at some point in their lives, or perhaps gradually over time, they realized that they had a choice. The point came at which they stopped watching what Jesus was doing from a distance and wanted to accept the invitation to be with Him and do what He was doing no matter the cost. These people decided they were not victims of circumstances or even acute suffering in this life, but they were empowered or, better yet, endowed with power from their heavenly Father to choose to be victorious in Christ Himself.

"Oh, but Parker, you have no idea what I have been through. I don't have *time* to pray and be with the Lord. I can't simply make a *choice* to keep these so-called internal promises. My circumstances are indeed unique and special."

Yes, you're right. Nobody's circumstances are anything like your circumstances. It is highly likely, though, that someone less intelligent than you, with less opportunity and graver circumstances, has served Christ in a capacity that would earn them glory in heaven beyond our greatest imagination. Yes, I said glory, and I mean it. Someone worse off than you at some point in history made the choice that they indeed have a choice—no matter the circumstances life and the devil throw at them. No matter what came their way, the choice had already been made. In fact, they were already dead.

Perhaps I've gotten ahead of myself here and come on a little too strong. But you'll get used to that.

The point is you always have a choice.

But first you have to make a much larger decision.

Refuse to be a victim even though you have been or will be victimized. Your lack of privilege is not the real problem. Someone else is not your problem at all. You will choose to no longer participate in the victim Olympics that our society has so skillfully brainwashed you into thinking holds some kind of prize.

The church hurt you? No kidding, it has people in it.

Your parents didn't raise you right? Of course they didn't. They are parents, and they didn't really know what they were doing, to be honest. I can tell you from firsthand knowledge that parenting is just constant learning and keeping young children in the dark, thinking that everything is going to be fine.

Abused? Yep. Unfortunately, it is completely normal in our world. Doesn't make it right; doesn't make it hurt less. Unfortunately, "abused" is not an identity in the Kingdom of God. You must refuse to let the person who abused you have that kind of power over the life God desires for you to have.

I grew up pretty far from rich. Right on the railroad tracks, literally. I was raised in a Christian cult until the age of 12. You want to talk about church hurt? Lord, have mercy. When I find the courage to write that book, I promise it will sell better than this one. I left everything I knew at 17 to move to California. I slept on the floor my senior year of high school (I kept rolling off the couch). My girlfriend cheated on me. I was lonely and cruising through a life filled with gray shapes. There was no color, and the light was veiled at best. With this "wonderful" church experience as a context for my future, I could have claimed that I really should stay away altogether—that the pain involved in the circumstances of my upbringing in church had left me no choice, that life had "dealt me a bad hand." I could have held on to bitterness and resentment. That was not the choice I made.

You can imagine what kind of life this produced in me. The answer? None at all. Feeling sorry for myself was a kind of drug that made me feel a certain way and feel nothing at all. It seems idiotic when I look back on it, but hindsight is, as we know, 20/20. I was feeling and focusing on things in order not to feel. Sounds like early stage depression? Sure does. That is what feeling sorry for yourself produces.

That is when everything truly changed. To say it better, it came to a point where it had to change. I did not want to live this way any longer, and desperation became my fuel. With all of this swirling around me, a choice still had to be made—or perhaps it is better stated as a response.

I was standing in the shower at 18 years old, suddenly weeping. Then the presence of Christ met me there the moment I asked. I thought this would be the time when I got to claim my victim status and live from a place where my anger and frustration were justified. To abandon the church and leave it all behind, live how I pleased, and forget everything that had to do with God.

But Jesus saved me, and when He did the excuses evaporated.

I couldn't cry anymore. That's when the decision was decisively made. I realized that even if I was indeed a victim in some cases, the life of a victim was not an option for me. There was one truly innocent victim, and He was a perfect man who went to the cross to save me.

I had an academic scholarship of sorts to a state university at the time. I gave the money back. I moved to Australia to start Bible college. The call came and I answered.

Here was the problem I began to run into. Before that moment when God had truly rescued me, I could live life as a victim. The circumstances and situations surrounding me I could blame on the external forces working against me. But no longer. I'd been saved, and if I read the Bible honestly, there was no way out. Someone who knows the truth of the saving power of Jesus is no longer a victim but an overcomer, despite what their eyes see. I could no longer blame the world, girls, the devil, or any circumstance for what my life would be.

I had a choice.

You may be angry at this point. You didn't have a choice with what life has dealt you at the great poker table of life. You may be angry that "fate" or even God Himself has given you a bad hand (or so you believe). Good, at least now we are feeling something worth feeling. Find out why you are mad and offended and take it to your King. This anger is one way to look at it, but measure well what it produces. Bitter seeds produce bitter fruit.

Let's make a point with a short story that I hope helps you and perhaps provides a small amount of conviction (or whatever measure you require) to change your perspective.

Aleksandr Solzhenitsyn was a commander fighting on the eastern front of World War II for the Soviet Union. He had endured what would be unimaginable hardship to most of us. The Russian soldier in World War II was accustomed to privation and suffering. The Soviets had bodies but were lacking in logistical excellence, to say the least. At times, they sent soldiers to take German positions with one rifle for every two men. You can imagine they were assuming that at least half would die, so there would be plenty of rifles on the ground to continue the advance.

As all soldiers tend to do at times, Aleksandr wrote a note with a few lines of complaint about Stalin, then leader of the Soviet Union. This letter was read, as many wartime

letters are, by intelligence officers and higher ranking offi-
cials so that no intelligence that would harm the war effort
would be sent away in the mail. In his current context,
even light criticism of Stalin was unwise, to say the least.

After years of fighting a brutal war, he was shipped off in
a truck to a gulag in Siberia—one of the harshest regions
in the world—for a ten-year sentence of hard labor. He
wrote about this in detail in his book *The Gulag Archipelago,* which every person should read. In great detail he
talks about his false trial, the dystopian prison he was first
shipped to, and in which he was tortured brutally before
being shipped off to a work camp in Siberia.

Over those ten years he experienced horror that is
unimaginable to the majority of us. Privation, murder,
rape, internal gangs, brutal sub-zero cold, corrupt and blatantly sadistic guards, and worst of all, the hopelessness
that haunts your mind with the prospect of an unknown
future and possibly worse things to come.

Here is the part that boggles the mind and indeed
the human spirit itself. The man remembered what
he went through and wrote a detailed account, which
in many respects toppled the Soviet Union. Here is a
quote from *The Gulag Archipelago* that distinctly describes
his attitude:

> If…if…We didn't love freedom enough. And
> even more—we had no awareness of the real
> situation…We purely and simply deserved
> everything that happened afterward.

He comes to the unbelievable conclusion that they deserved it—that he deserved it. After ten years of what could only be described as hell, he realized something that set him free. It was his fault. He should have spoken the truth sooner, should not have let the little lies pile up. He was responsible for his own imprisonment. The only responsibility for his life lay squarely on himself.

Now, you may not have been traumatized or victimized as a coherent and capable adult as he was; perhaps you were a child. No matter what happened then, the fact of the matter is that now you have a choice. It may be painful, as life so often is, but that isn't the point. You can actually set others free by making the choice to use the manure pile of circumstances and the dumpster fire of choices you previously made to make the world a better place. What is the very first step to being victorious? Take a thorough account of your life, lay it before Christ, and take responsibility for it. This is where the magic happens.

You can be free, and you can be victorious. The rub of it all is that it's your choice whether you are or not.

You picked this book up knowing that it was about spiritual disciplines. Good. That is an excellent start. That means you are willing to do something to find the path to victory. You are making another promise by doing that, though. This cannot be just another book you read. You have to get so absolutely fed up with a "normal" Christian life that it makes you sick. That it repels you. That you, like Christ, choose right now to spew it out of your mouth.

Until you are ready to do this—to commit to seeking victory, to seeking true heavenly glory that Christ promises us—put this book down and pray until you receive it. Because once you start reading, once you see the ancient way of Christ that has led so many down a path to true heavenly glory, you'll be accountable to it. It will stick in your mind like a Swedish pop song or a child's viral YouTube video until you put it on the radio in the car, by yourself, and sing it out until it's finished so you can finally have some mental peace.

You will know the truth, and it will set you free.

If you choose not to follow the path, it will haunt you as it did the rich young ruler. As it did me in my teenage years.

Jesus so blatantly says, "I am the Way, I am the Truth, I am the Life, and *nobody* comes to the Father but by *Me*."

Are you ready to make the choice to walk The Path?

The Path

In the space provided, meditate on these scriptures and make your choice. Will you continue to sit among those who have all of God available to them, yet choose the mundane, sidelined, victimized life? Or will you stand among those who have endured to the end, who choose to live in victory *despite* overwhelming circumstances and the poor choices of those who have wounded them?

Write out and repent of the ways you have been living as a victim and an orphan. Then commit, with a signature and date, that by the grace given to you, you will choose to become victorious.

Now take some time and write down all the things holding you back from pursuing God and walking in the way of discipleship. What keeps tripping you up? What excuses do you keep making? What pain, past or present, has driven you away from going toward Him?

Write these down and write them in detail. Share these with someone close to you who is walking with Christ—a wife, a pastor, a mentor. Now hand them to Christ to deal with. Perhaps your pain won't disappear, but never let these things be excuses again; let them be lessons. Make your choice here and commit to walking out a new life, no matter how imperfect it may be. Correct your aim and turn it forward instead of backward—forward toward Christ.

> *And I heard a loud voice in heaven, saying, "Now the salvation and the power and the kingdom of our God and the authority of his Christ have come, for the accuser of our brothers has been thrown down, who accuses them day and night before our God. And they have conquered him by the blood of the Lamb and by the word of their testimony, for they loved not their lives even unto death" (Revelation 12:10-11 ESV).*
>
> *What then shall we say to these things? If God is for us, who can be against us? He who did not spare his own Son but gave him up for us all, how will he not also with him graciously give us all things? Who shall bring any charge against God's*

elect? It is God who justifies. Who is to condemn? Christ Jesus is the one who died—more than that, who was raised—who is at the right hand of God, who indeed is interceding for us. Who shall separate us from the love of Christ? Shall tribulation, or distress, or persecution, or famine, or nakedness, or danger, or sword? As it is written,

"For your sake we are being killed all the day long; we are regarded as sheep to be slaughtered."

No, in all these things we are more than conquerors through him who loved us. For I am sure that neither death nor life, nor angels nor rulers, nor things present nor things to come, nor powers, nor height nor depth, nor anything else in all creation, will be able to separate us from the love of God in Christ Jesus our Lord (Romans 8:31-39 ESV).

Signature line

Chapter 3

BEYOND SELF

There was a day when I died, utterly died—died to George Müller, his opinions, preferences, tastes, and will; died to the world, its approval or censure; died to the approval or blame even of my brethren and friends—and since then I have only to show myself approved to God.
—George Müller

Imagine being truly free, with everything to live for and nothing to lose. That's what getting beyond self really looks like. However, there is only one path that we can take to that place. Jesus shows us that our desires, our life, what we really want may not, in fact, be what we wanted at all. That the self-focused life only leads to the insane level of depression, anxiety, greed, envy, sexual perversion—I could go on. When we see Jesus for who He is, we can get beyond ourselves and get to the life that we long for. Laying eyes on Him will change you forever, if you are willing to see. It will make you seem like a madman, an extremist, a revolutionary. Perhaps you know there is more to it all than living trapped in your own mind, thinking about your own problems and your own worldly success. It's inevitable that you will have both of these in your life, but what will they do to *you* as a person? How will you respond to the roar of the crowd? To abandonment and betrayal?

You can respond by simply following Jesus and what He did with both public accolade and bitter betrayal. The secret kept before the foundation of the world between Him and the Father—that he would die for the sins of the world—meant that He was a man living as though dead. I would suggest that, aside from the fact that He is completely divine, the humanity of Him surely would have been tempted by immediate power when He was popular, and to sulk and play the victim when he was abandoned. Instead, he faced it all with resolve for his mission to literally save the world.

Let's meditate on the fact that Jesus is the only person in all of human history who actually could have claimed complete injustice and laid hold of the victim status that is sought after like a prize in our society, but He did not. Jesus stated very clearly that nobody took His life from Him, that He laid it down of His own accord. No popularity or deep betrayal could touch Him.

No one takes it from me, but I lay it down of my
own accord. I have authority to lay it down, and
I have authority to take it up again. This charge I
have received from my Father (John 10:18 ESV).

He who wants to save his life shall lose it. Jesus showed us that first.

Have you ever met someone who is overwhelmingly peaceful in the midst of chaos? Someone who has an absolute presence to the point where nothing around them can affect their direction or identity? It carries weight in a room.

I have maybe twice in my life, and I deeply desired that gift. There is a certain violence to it that moves against the tide of our frenetic world. A peace that almost surrounds them like a shield. No matter what someone says about them, whether praise or slander, they seem unmoved. This was the way of Jesus, and it should be ours too.

The secret is this—you have to die.

You are no longer the central character in this movie.

This is a hard statement to hear, and it's even more difficult in practice. What does dying to yourself actually look like? How does someone "practice" this to stay on the narrow path? Well, the reality is it actually does take daily practice to put our own fleshly desires aside and let them die, truly let them burn, and go on to produce fruit in keeping with repentance.

Baptism is a good physical example of this. You are stepping into some container of water, be it a beautiful baptismal, a cattle trough, or your own bathtub, being witnessed by your new family in Christ. It is a literal picture of your flesh and old man dying and the new one being raised to life in Christ. It is not just a metaphor or a traditional practice but a tangible spiritual event that lays to rest the dead things, the dead you, and brings to life the new creation in Jesus.

How does baptism kill the flesh? How is this death to self? To begin with, it simply does not make sense to the logical mind, "Well, of course I should be fully immersed in water if I am a repentant sinner in need of Christ; this is completely logical." You are doing something spiritual by acting through your physical body—you are being led by the Spirit of God by first being convicted by Him, then led into death, and then sonship.

> *And when he comes, he will convict the world concerning sin and righteousness and judgment: concerning sin, because they do not believe in me; concerning righteousness, because I go to the Father, and you will see me no longer; concerning judgment, because the ruler of this world is judged* (John 16:8-11 ESV).

The Mundane Is Miraculous

Here is another example of daily practice from my life. I have dreams, aspirations, desires of my heart that I have written about for years in my various journals. I certainly want to be an influence, to be honored among my peers, to stand at the end of my life and have no regrets. This is a mental image that I project onto myself, and if I am not careful, it fills me with pride even before this is accomplished in my life. Do you want to guess what brings me quickly down to earth? The mundane duties of life.

Most of your life will be filled with seemingly average tasks. Nothing feels more average when you are full of fleshly pride than housework and tending to little children. The almost hilarious part of it all is that this is enormously important to God Himself—these (seemingly) secret practices of constantly dying. Will I give my wife attention when I am consumed with a project? Will I tend to a disappointed or enthusiastic and talkative son? Will I empty the garbage for (God forbid) the *second* time that day? Will I wake early in order to minister to the Lord, even if it's an ungodly hour, in order that I may lead my family well?

There is an almost hilarious paradox between preaching the gospel—seeing miracles take place, being honored in random locations for gifts and character—and your kids literally not giving the slightest thought to it, thinking it's normal, and only truly caring about who you are to *them*. The presence you bring to the table. Are you there? Or are you living in a fantasy that is either past or future? Those are two places you simply cannot live.

Many times the dying happens by simply living in reality right where you are. Like other things that are part of our new nature in Christ, this takes practice. Changing a diaper or anything comparable to it brings your feet down to earth immediately.

In truth, none of these things are very physically or even mentally difficult, but they directly challenge our self-will. This is the root of unrighteous anger—someone or something stepping in the way of your will, or what the stoics would call your ego. The self-inflated version of yourself that thinks it is more inherently valuable than the people around you and more central to the world's ultimate purpose than God's will itself. This is the part of us that rages against God, and this is especially the part that needs to die.

You Won't Find Anything of Use by "Finding Yourself"

This is where the initial fall (see Adam and Eve) tried to rip God from the true center of all things good. We made ourselves the center of what was good and what was evil. This is what caused Adam and Eve to hide themselves from God and cover themselves with fig leaves. They were ultimately aware that they made a mistake. Our ego is an ignorant response to this decision of rebellion. In order to avoid guilt, we make ourselves judge, jury, and executioner, whether physically, mentally, or especially with our words. This is the projected ego—who we think we are. Unfortunately, a false self set on false pretense mixed in a witch's brew of twisted truth and our fallen nature produces literal hell on earth for ourselves and those around us.

The flip side of this metaphorical and metaphysical coin is that if you let the Holy Spirit convict you, go to the cross, and carry it daily, the ego—the fleshly, worldly man—starves and dies. When he does, your feet are firmly planted in a spiritual reality that actually gives you power to live out the gospel in your daily life. Without fear of man, without fear of the future, and without anxiety about "who you are." For who you are is dead and everything you are is in Christ eternally sealed by the Holy Spirit. You are wrapped up in the eternal God; you are truly in a place of complete belonging and safety. This makes you unstoppable. Let the dead things die, let the unregenerate you be buried, and get free to be victorious on the path of life.

There is a scene that lays this out well in one of my favorite shows of all time, *Band of Brothers*. There is a sizeable contingent of Nazis faced off against an American Airborne Company (for those of us who went to public school, that's World War II). They are each staying in their respective hedgerows, hundreds of yards apart, waiting for the real fighting to break out. At dawn on the morning after they arrive, the Airborne unit takes the offensive. During this early morning attack, there is one private in his foxhole, paralyzed with fear, unable to move or even fire his weapon in the right direction. In this terrifying moment, Lieutenant Speirs, standing over the foxhole seemingly impervious to German rounds, looks down at the man trembling in his foxhole and lays down my favorite quote of the show:

> The only hope you have is to accept the fact that you're already dead. The sooner you accept that, the sooner you'll be able to function as a soldier is supposed to function…all war depends upon it.

Memento Mori: Remember, You'll Die

Too many Christians believe they are going to get out of this thing alive. As soon as we can accept the fact that we are already dead to ourselves and to the world itself, we can function well as soldiers enlisted to continue the mission of Jesus and save the world. You are going to die physically, and it's a good thing to remember, but what I'm talking about is something that we practice daily.

Death to self.

This is how we truly go beyond ourselves, our petty needs, the worldly things we hold on to, and our deeply embedded desire for survival and accumulation. We must go beyond ourselves by laying down every aspect of our lives, laying it before the King, and giving Him absolute permission to burn it. Painful, yes, but absolutely necessary to be everything that God is calling us to.

We wander through this life with half-hearted desires— to survive, to live, to get by. So much of this is because of the fall of man; it's in your nature. Still, there is something else about our natures that is in the deepest part of who we are, the very center of our being:

> It would seem that Our Lord finds our desires not too strong, but too weak. We are half-hearted creatures, fooling about with drink and sex and ambition when infinite joy is offered us, like an ignorant child who wants to go on making mud pies in a slum because he cannot imagine what is meant by

the offer of a holiday at the sea. We are far too easily pleased.

—C.S. LEWIS, "The Weight of Glory"

In every single one of us, there is a desire to have something worth dying for so that we can truly live. It's what we are all searching for. What if you knew beyond a shadow of a doubt, with everything in you, that the hope you have in Christ was worth laying it all down for, including your own life? This is what freedom looks like. It looks like a Christian soldier with a mind of steel and a heart of flesh, unattached to the things of this world that push and pull on him in every direction. Truthful in the face of catastrophe, loving in the face of humiliation, full of hope amidst a hopeless situation, holy and set apart in a world of shattered morality.

We have to go beyond the self-care mentality that pervades our world. It's gone beyond rest and recovery of the soul as it should be; it has become a trap to become completely self-focused and prideful. We do not have the time in this short life for an inflated ego. For most of us, that is what needs to die first.

Be Dangerous

I heard a great story from Bill Johnson. He was spending time with the mayor of his city. They were heading into a coffee shop, and a woman barked something rude at the mayor, cut him off, and cut in line. Bill asked him why he didn't respond more aggressively. He simply said, "I can afford it."

You see, when we operate as dead to sin and alive to Christ, we can afford it as well. Whether it be a family member or a random person in traffic—we can afford it. The price has been paid for us, our ledger is clear, we're dead already. We have our hope in awaiting the return of Christ, resurrection, and the restoration of all things.

Once we realize the life we have in Christ, we realize we have nothing to lose.

Be careful here, because when you become this type of person, you become dangerous. You see it blatantly clear in the life of Jesus and His apostles. All except for one were martyred. You may be too, because everything that the world is telling you to do is the opposite of following Christ. To leave selfishness and ego behind and choose to die every single day is a decision to be an opposing and offensive force against the power of the flesh, the world, and the devil. You will stand out against the crowd in a sea of brokenness. You'll be a light shining in absolute darkness. In short, you will be a Christian.

As we go through this book, we're going to learn lots of ways to die. The great part about it is you'll actually finally get to live. Just look at the words of Jesus:

> *Whoever finds his life will lose it, and whoever loses his life for my sake will find it* (Matthew 10:39 ESV).

In order to truly find life, you have to lose it. Everyone has to start somewhere, and we know that's what the disciples did too. You simply have to make a start.

The Path

Let's get right to the nitty gritty.

What is *one* way, in the next 30 days, that you can shoulder the load of your cross that would radically change your life and the lives of those around you? Write a list, if need be, then narrow it down to the one that would affect change in the most aspects of your walk with Christ. Then share this with your spouse, good friend, and/or spiritual leadership and commit to being open to them for feedback on how you're doing it. If you don't have any of those relationships, that goes on the list, starting with spiritual leadership.

Chapter 4

THE FREEDOM OF DISCIPLINE

Discipline equals freedom.
—JOCKO WILLINK

Never has the church been more in need of true freedom as defined by scripture. Never has it been understood less. In ministry over the past three years, I have seen more deliverance from evil spirits than in my almost-20 years of ministry combined. Not just this, but many are held in self-destructive habits, some of them even spiritual or charismatic in nature. Be wary of any Christian from any denomination who tells you what they do has been ordained by God but does not produce fruit in keeping with repentance.

Christians in massive numbers are oppressed by evil spirits and habits of the flesh that continually open the door to the thoughts and practices of our enemy. But you may argue, "Christians are filled with the Holy Spirit; they cannot be possessed by an unclean spirit, can they?" Well, you can tell me what you know. I will tell you what I have seen.

In a small field next to the Red River Meeting House in Kentucky, I was standing next to our security detail as ministry began to break out during baptisms at one of our Saturate revival meetings. No more than 50 feet away I heard a guttural growl that made the hair on the back of my neck stand up. The security detail (a contractor and a Baptist, not a charismatic) looked at me with raised eyebrows and said, "That's not a person."

I ventured over to where a group of people had gathered to minister to this young lady; she was weighing in at maybe 120 pounds soaking wet. Four women were attempting to hold her down as she screamed and growled. I assisted, held her in place, and began to pray. Whatever it was that had possessed her looked me in the eyes, and to this day I still remember it as an imprint on my mind. I had never seen such pure, unadulterated hatred for me personally. My wife and I eventually worked together with our team to see this young woman get freedom. She had been going to church, been saved, etc. But I realized at the back end of all that, she had failed to form the habits of her life into Christ, and this was leaving the door open for deep oppression. She had raised her hand and said the prayer, but she was bound.

Grace Empowers Your Effort

Perhaps our myriad issues and habits—self-destruction, habitual sin, flying off the handle, struggling with depression, anxiety, and eating disorders—are spiritual in nature first. Luckily, they have an immediate and long-term spiritual solution.

We must first understand why spiritual disciplines even matter. Many would say this kind of talk is a gospel of works and not grace. However, as Dallas Willard so keenly says, "Grace is not opposed to effort, it is opposed to earning."[1] All this to say, if you truly desire to live a life of freedom, you must have a heart as soft as clay and a body and mind as hard as steel. This is not some game you have stepped into; it is a fight, and literally a fight for your life and future generations. Casual Christianity is no Christianity at all. Random kindness, random love, random Bible study, random fasting, random prayer, random generosity, random victory—these are things that simply do not exist. They all take focused effort and practice and are never accidental. The life of a believer is intentionally aimed at forming us into the image of Christ so that the good works that you do may give glory to your Father in heaven (see Matthew 5:16).

Before we get down to brass tacks on the spiritual disciplines, which if practiced will indeed teach you to overcome and be victorious, I'd like to say a couple of things about what has been called spiritual formation.

Practice Makes Permanent

First of all, this is not a book on spiritual formation as it is currently defined. You can have the appearance of good, even with spiritual disciplines, and still be a whitewashed tomb. I am not telling you to be a monk or quit your job and hide in a cave or ignore your crying child or emotionally or sexually deprived spouse because you are so "holy and disciplined." If your wife needs a listening ear, it's probably not time to pray. If your husband wants to make love, don't make a spiritual excuse—God is not in competition with your husband. This is the opposite, in almost every case, of the purpose of spiritual disciplines. The purpose is, more correctly, that you become the *type* of person who responds proactively to life in a Christ-like manner.

- Getting berated by a boss, friend, or spouse? Good, you've already practiced silence.

- Feeling alone in pioneering? Good, you've been alone before; you've practiced.

- Broke and not sure how to pay the bills? Good, you've practiced generosity.

- Huge financial windfall? Good, you've practiced generosity and frugality. You don't need things; you need more of Him.

- Someone spreading rumors about you at work and/or church? Good, you know how to pray for them.

- Sexual and emotional temptation when your marriage isn't ideal? Good, you've practiced fasting, and if you can stop eating you can stop anything.

- Huge opportunity came your way? Good, you've been in the secret place with the King daily, and you know who gave this promotion to you, so there is no reason to fear mortal man.

- Someone tells you you'll lose your job if you stand by Christ and His word? Good, you've already practiced dying daily.

You see, these are tools to be applied to your life so that you may have *real* victory. Let's define victory from scripture. Revelation 12:10-11 (ESV) says:

> *And I heard a loud voice in heaven, saying, "Now the salvation and the power and the kingdom of our God and the authority of his Christ have come, for the accuser of our brothers has been thrown down, who accuses them day and night before our God. And they have conquered him by the blood of the Lamb and by the word of their testimony, for they loved not their lives even unto death."*

I want this book to be a weapon in your arsenal that makes you an effective disciple. A witness of the gospel. A dead one who is raised to life in Christ. A truly free person. A free people are a dangerous people. The cause of much of the church's impotence in our century has been the fact that we simply are not free, but we think that we are. We may be independent, religious, intelligent, skilled and still be slaves to sin and useless habits that hold us back.

James makes it clear: *"But be doers of the word, and not hearers only, deceiving yourselves"* (James 1:22 ESV).

So why would spiritual disciplines lead to freedom? Because we forget the opposing hand of freedom—the thumb of freedom, as I like to call it—that allows you to actually get a firm grip on it. Like a car without an engine, so is freedom without responsibility. It is stagnant and useless, even if the paint and interior are absolute perfection. Freedom is a gift that has been given to us by the work and victory of Christ, and we are now responsible and without excuse to use that freedom as Jesus intends.

All of this discipline is aimed at one particular thing. To say it better, it's aimed at getting nearer to a Person.

All true discipleship produces intimacy with Christ and obedience to Him. If this is not the fruit, then your aim is off and you need to reassess what you are doing. Practice tends toward permanence, not perfection. But if you learn to aim for "the perfect" who is Christ, the habits, attitudes, and results of your life will begin to more *permanently* look like Him.

This is not a book on navel gazing and spiritual tinkering. This is a field manual for overcoming in private and in public. Practice, after all, is done many times in the dark so that when the lights are shining, when the heat is cranked up to inferno temperature, you can say like the great apostle, *"I have fought the good fight, I have finished the race, I have kept the faith"* (2 Timothy 4:7 ESV).

I quoted one of my favorite current podcast hosts at the top of this chapter, and I hope you can adopt what he is saying. Jocko Willink is a former Navy Seal who saw combat in Iraq and is an author, successful businessman, and generally a dangerous human being. As far as I can tell from reading his books and listening to his podcast, the phrase means that when you are disciplined in life, life tends to supply far more opportunity. In warfare, a highly disciplined army, even if it is a smaller force, has the advantage. Why? Because the things an untrained and undisciplined fighter has to think about, they do by knee-jerk, instant reaction. When the pressure is on they rise, not because of the moment, but because they are falling to the level of their training. This allows for creative thinking, for mobility, for decision making, for the power to overcome obstacles. When the heat is on, they can think to themselves, "I've already been here a thousand times."

You're Already at War, So You Might as Well Practice

When Julius Caesar invaded Gaul he took with him four legions. A legion would consist of somewhere between 3,000-5,000 soldiers depending on the period. At best, he had 20,000 soldiers. He invaded a tribal land called Gaul (modern-day France) while deeply in debt and in need of victory. The forces arrayed against him under the command of Vercingetorix, a tribal chieftain, were somewhere between 80,000-100,000. The Gauls were ferocious, had flair and vigor in battle, were considered physically quite large for the time, and had superior numbers. After years of campaigning, the Romans decisively defeated the Gauls at Alesia.

What was their secret to overcoming the overwhelming odds stacked against them? Discipline. They didn't scatter or showboat, and they fought as a disciplined unit. Untrained soldiers will run away in panic, step over each other for perceived glory, not know their place or context on the battlefield, be unable to follow practiced commands, and generally not hold a line. The Romans knew what to do and had disciplined logistics to supply them, which meant they were eating when their enemy was starving.

Although the numbers are likely inflated by the victorious Caesar, the story tells a tale. A small, disciplined force is better than even a massive, overwhelming, disorganized, and unpracticed force.

The same goes for spiritual conflict. The reason we suffer so much as a church in this era is that we don't hear the command of Christ in the midst of a fight, because we haven't been with Him. We don't know how to counter false ideology because we neither study nor live the word. We have rampant sin in the pulpit because talent and flair have been honored over character. We lose the pioneering spirit because we have never learned to be alone.

These spiritual practices strengthen us in the presence of God to fight properly. Not as a boxer beating the air, but with distinct purpose (see 1 Corinthians 9:25-27). When the enemy does invade our lives, when circumstances are difficult or busy and thrilling, we must be disciplined in our response so that we take decisive action and make forward progress against our enemy. Your "Christianity" must survive contact with the enemy. And as life is unpredictable, your best laid plans are many times fantasy compared to the reality you're dealing with. All you have in that moment of decision is how well you have practiced being with and living like Jesus.

The practice of our faith both in secret and in public has a purpose. That is to make us like Jesus so that when any and all situations arise in our lives we can be the type of people who respond like Him no matter the circumstance.

The Path

Every athlete exercises self-control in all things. They do it to receive a perishable wreath, but we an imperishable. So I do not run aimlessly; I do not box as one beating the air. But I discipline my body and keep it under control, lest after preaching to others I myself should be disqualified (1 Corinthians 9:25-27 ESV).

Write this passage of scripture down in a place where you will see it every day. Read it repeatedly until it becomes a part of you.

What is one area of your life, just one, that you can focus your aim on and begin to practice daily? This does not have to be "spiritual." Just pick something and stick to it. You'll find that this gives you more freedom in your daily life. Discipline always makes discipline babies, and nothing is done in a vacuum. What that means is that the basic disciplines of following Jesus affect everything else. Habit is most of what you do; make them good habits.

Note

1. Dallas Willard, *The Great Omission* (New York, NY: HarperCollins, 2006), 61.

Chapter 5

THE SECRET TO LIFE

But he would withdraw to desolate places and pray.
—LUKE 5:16 ESV

The two largest struggles of our generation are described in two simple but complex questions.

Who am I?

What am I supposed to do?

The unfortunate outcome has been people searching for answers and following nonsense with no point of reference whatsoever. God has been removed from the picture altogether as "experts" talk on and on about the complexity of these questions without providing an answer that actually leads to life, and life more abundantly. This is what every human being is really searching for in the end—a life that is actually "life," after all. In almost every hall of academia, in the media, even in our own homes human frailty and fallenness has been on full display. The result has been death. Not simply physically, like depression that leads to suicide and self-harm, but the death of the human spirit. We are like zombies devouring each other in order to gain sustenance from one another's purpose and identity.

Sadly, the church has not been left unharmed by this flood of expert opinion and manmade wisdom. As much as it can be a useful tool for the gospel, social media has also presented the problem of creating an end-all-be-all of Christian living that is at best a highlight reel and at worst an outright lie. A generation of young people are growing up without a true center in the gospel (and without fathers, but that's another book). They are picking up whatever possible scraps they can from 60-second tutorials on worshiping and following the God of the universe.

So what is to be done? Better yet, what should you do?

I'll make this as simple as possible: our purpose is to know Christ and to obey Him.

This phrase is the core of all discipleship.

Who are we? We are who we are only in proper relation to Christ.

Let me explain.

The God of all the universe makes humankind in His image; humankind sins and decides to rule over themselves; horror, multiplied sin, and death follow. Jesus, the perfect

God-man, comes to earth to save us by sacrifice, redeem us by His resurrection by defeating death itself, ascends to heaven to rule and send the Spirit by which we continue His reign, and promises to return to perfect all things. You can only understand who you are through this brutally abbreviated story of God's relation to humankind. When we make ourselves the center of the story, we spin out of control with no gravity and with no context for our place in the universe.

What, then, should we do? The same story tells us. Everything went disastrously wrong when we stepped out from under God's authority and made our own way.

When Jesus lived His life, He made two things abundantly clear. His relationship to His Father was the most important thing in the universe, and obeying Him was inseparable from this relationship. This is the path that we need to follow. Indeed, our hearts are crying out for it; yours is right now in this very moment. Every bad habit, every sin that makes you feel something, every romantic relationship you give too much importance, and all the weighty religious practice is you simply trying to feel alive. The central issue is that only God can do that. Our lives only make sense in *relation* to Him.

A person who knows who they are and knows where they are going is dangerous to the kingdom of darkness. More than that, this person is so full of life that they become fearless. This is the root of our belief in Christ. This right relation to Him as King, as Lord, as friend, as God is the way that we find our anchor and true purpose in life.

Getting Away with God

There is something about being truly *away*, whether it's being next to a flowing mountain stream in the Sierra Nevada, on a beach in Mexico, or even in a room where you know for certain that you won't have the interruptions of life invade your space.

When I went for the first time to the mountains in Southern California, I was in the midst of one of those seasons when life simply would not stop pressing in, and I had to get away. So I packed up some camping gear, some cans of chili, and a few pounds of ground beef into my '83 Honda Accord hatchback, picked a spot on a map, and just drove. This was over ten years ago, so I don't remember if I had a printed map or Google. What I do know is that my phone stopped working about five hours into the drive. Steering along the one-lane mountain road up what seemed like the jagged spine of Sequoia National Park, I began to feel the weight of the world slip off of my body. It was as if some sort of magnet held all my problems and angst against the valley floor; the higher I climbed and the taller the pines got, the more free I felt. I was going to find God on a mountain, in October, in a desolate place.

I did not know where I was. I had never been there before, but I knew where I was going. Those few days truly alone (I saw another person on the third day) have set the course for the secret of all spiritual disciplines—the secret place.

Many times there was so much buildup of life, the weight of the daily grind or of sins committed, and general worldliness that it took the long drive just to get me to a place where I could truly focus on Him.

When I moved to New York in 2012, the need for this time became something far beyond casual. I had a real ministry job for the first time. Those of you who know, know. I had been a volunteer for ten years at this point in two different churches. I couldn't just escape to the mountains when I felt like it or spend hours with God when work was slow like I had when I was a personal trainer. There was a job to be done.

The getaways were good and necessary, but eventually it seemed the results would peter out and I just needed to get back to the mountains again. When I was in New York, that simply wasn't an available option. To add to this, a wife and children entered the scene—all of this was a blessing—although the option to just go away when I felt like it simply no longer existed. I was now responsible for a growing family. So I took drastic measures in order to meet with Him. For almost three years now (except for the newborn phases, to be honest) I have been waking between 4 a.m. and 5 a.m. every morning in order to be with Jesus. Luckily, by the time I had children, the "muscle" for it was already there. Yes, it was hard at first. I simply had to decide what was truly important to me. I decided I could not live without Him, so, following Jesus' example in scripture, I got up before the sun.

> *And rising very early in the morning, while it was still dark, he departed and went out to a desolate place, and there he prayed* (Mark 1:35 ESV).

Rising early began a long journey of continuing to seek that place of solitude with Jesus. Both in the mountains and in rooms, closets, bathrooms (I have three kids), empty church sanctuaries, and long car rides. I began to crave it—the time spent with just me and Him, the Creator and lover of my soul. I realized that it didn't just "center" me and put me in my proper place on this earth; it made me come alive.

I found that the secret place was *the* cornerstone habit, *the discipline* that begets all other spiritual disciplines. Without this fundamental practice, the rest of your walk will fall apart. You cannot be silent, fast, pray, study scripture, be truly generous, reach the lost, or defeat lust and fantasy without this. Every single one of these things is done within the practice of the presence of God.

I won't say, "Don't skip this step," because this is not a step. It is the deep excavation that is dug in the ground and into which the concrete is poured before the true edifice is built. It may take you months just to get into this habit properly, just like it takes months to build a foundation to a truly impressive structure. You can look at it this way so your impatience doesn't get the better of you. We have to remember that digging is building, just like plowing and planting is farming, even if you're not yet harvesting.

The Foundation Is the Building

While living and ministering in New York, our church had an office building in the financial district with multiple skyscrapers that surrounded us. Our neighbor building, though, was a dump of a parking garage in disuse. A few months into our church leasing that office, the parking garage was demolished and excavation began. Down and down it went. We had a good view from the bathroom window, so when I took the occasional "relief break" I would check their progress. From my vast experience in high density skyscraper construction, things seemed to be going well, if you were into large chasms. This took months—almost eight months, from what I recall. Then all of a sudden, the structure started to go up, and it went so fast in comparison to the previous groundwork that I could not keep track of the progress. Within the same amount of time it took to dig the foundation and lay the electric, plumbing, concrete, retaining walls etc., a huge apartment building was up and ready for renters.

This is what our secret place is—the foundation and connection that makes everything else work. We can only imagine, for that is all the gospels allow us to do, how much time Jesus spent in prayer and in the word before His ministry was public. Then, when His ministry was out in the open and He was on mission, He made this His priority. We, broken and twisted as we are in our habits and desires, need this even more. This is not an excuse to forgo ministering, or to pause being a witness of the gospel, or to pull back from great risks of faith. It is, however, a simple spiritual reality. Without a foundation you will fall at the first hardship, storm, or great success achieved, which is a tempest of its own kind.

Now I want to show you how you can practice this yourself and see the deepest parts of your life truly be redeemed in your walk with Christ.

Before we begin the practical portion of this chapter, I want to highlight the fact that nothing is more practical than being with Jesus. He says, "I am the way, the truth, and the life." This is the answer, the secret. We are too often looking for a new habit or practice, and I understand the irony of that in a book about spiritual practice. This is the precise thing in your life that needs to be held in tension. All spiritual discipline is a way to Jesus, intimacy with Him, and obedience to Him. That should be the definition of discipline that guides you as a believer. All this crucifying of the flesh you will embark on as you continue to read this book is to be a person of the Spirit. A living, breathing epistle of Christ. A story written on your heart and in your life that leaves everything in pursuit of Him.

Again, discipleship is intimacy with Christ and obedience to Him. The first principle is to make space where you will meet God. You are a spiritual being, but you are not a gnostic being.[1]

Find a space. Yes, God is everywhere, but you are not. Your body is located right where you are, and the space you occupy matters. What you do with your physical body matters. Set it up in whatever way helps you focus. Keep in mind this is a muscle that needs exercise, a practice that needs consistency. At some point you will realize that the secret place can be anywhere at any time, no matter how stressed, nervous, or overwhelmed you may be. If you can't do it in the quiet of the morning, without distraction, then when the time comes to commune with God in a situation where you're being bombarded, you won't have what it takes to shift yourself, go on offense, commune with God, and substantially change the circumstances you are facing. Even better, simply be still and know He's God when all the demands of your life come knocking at the door.

Life does happen. For instance, if you're a woman with a baby less than six months old, you're going to be more tired than you have ever been in your life. That child needs you, and it's a marvelous and godly thing to care for it. I watched my wife do this with three children, and it can be difficult to find a rhythm in circumstances like this. Here, though, lies a secret—love finds a way. It won't ever be perfect, so it's better to start or continue in your imperfection than to not pursue Him at all. God is gracious and honors our feeble attempts and even makes our weakness glory when it's in Him.

Second, set aside time.

I often tell this little quip to the people I teach and disciple. Imagine Jesus is knocking on your door at 5 a.m. You have an appointment with Him; will you open the door? Will you be at the appointment?

Treat Jesus like a real person, as He is, and you will notice a radical change in your secret place. You will get the results of a real Jesus when you treat Him as a real person. It may sound redundant and even simple to the point of stupidity, but a real person needs to be honored as such. Honor your time by honoring Jesus with it.

Third, make a simple plan of some kind. The elements here are the ability to be silent, read and study the word, pray, and worship. Here is where most people end up losing the fight when they begin to practice the secret place. Why? They take on too much "weight." If you have never stepped into a weight room in your entire life or done hard labor and then decide one day to throw 315 pounds on the squat rack and have a go, you will realize quickly that you have made a life altering mistake. Confess your strength all you want, have good intentions about your strength, claim the grace of God and the strength of Samson over the barbell, let Philippians 4:13 stream from your mouth in praise and faithful expectation—you will still fail. Why? Because you haven't practiced and you didn't have a plan.

Start in the secret place with an amount of time that makes sense. Gradually work that muscle and rely on the grace of God to encourage you and sustain you in it. But do not make a plan that will crush you just as you're starting this discipline. Make a plan to lengthen your time with the Lord over a period of weeks. Keep the phone in a different room, write down your prayers, think and meditate on scripture, and stop as you read to let the passage roll over you.

Fundamentals first. Play scales before you play jazz.

Remember the whole point is to keep your heart and mind focused on Christ. Yes, we all have difficulty, but make sure you give that difficulty a heavenly perspective *first* by glorifying Christ above it all. You will find your problems aren't so oppressive, and that Jesus, being God, is in absolute control. The sense of peace that comes from this daily practice cannot be exaggerated and escapes all hyperbole. It is the rock solid foundation upon which all pursuit of spiritual disciplines is built. It will, in fact, be the cornerstone upon which you build your entire life. It can't be skipped, skirted, or done half-heartedly.

Lastly, make the appointment.

Choose a time when you will be in God's presence, in a secret place, without distraction, daily. Put it in your calendar. To reiterate, treat Jesus like a real person. Consistency is everything. The whole world understands the principle of compound interest, and it is no different in relationships. No discipline takes place in a vacuum apart from the rest of your life. In the end, the continual habit of the secret place will not add; it will multiply. At first you may feel like you are gathering spare change in a jar—that's good, at least you are learning. We all must be fools in order to be wise. In the end, though, you will begin to see the compounding take effect and have access to the riches of the presence of Christ that have no end.

There is always more of Him.

Make the space. Make the appointment. Make a plan.

The Path

Find or make a place where you can meet Jesus without distraction.

Make a Plan: How will you meet Him?

Put these in an order that works for the time and place you have chosen. And, however awkwardly, practice them.

- Silence
- Bible Reading and Study
- Worship
- Prayer

Set a Time: When will you meet Him?

Yes, put it in the calendar. You are a finite, created being and time is your most precious possession. Give it to Jesus and make it absolutely clear.

The best things are simple things. Some of the hardest things are simple things. Some balk at a plan to meet with Jesus as inorganic, or they might say, "I talk to God all the time." My personal perspective is that unless you are Enoch being carried away into the heavens as we speak, neither of those statements hold any truth. They are excuses to treat Jesus like a servant to our whims and our schedule and not the sole master of our life.

Just get started, and keep starting again every day until this is a natural part of your life.

Note

1. Gnosticism is the belief that human beings contain a piece of God (the highest good or a divine spark) within themselves, which has fallen from the immaterial world into the bodies of humans. All physical matter is subject to decay, rotting, and death." (Rebecca Denova, "Gnosticism," *World History Encyclopedia*, April 9, 2021, https://www.worldhistory.org/Gnosticism.) Gnostics believed that the human body was lesser than and unimportant. Yet a risen Christ in physical form points to this as a dangerous heresy that still lingers with us today. Christ rules in human, physical form at the right hand of the Father; He is perfect and inhabits a human body; we will be just like Him in the new heavens and the new earth. Your physical body matters to God.

Chapter 6

THE SWORD

In the beginning was the Word, and the Word
was with God, and the Word was God. He was
in the beginning with God. All things were made
through him, and without him was not any thing
made that was made. In him was life, and the life
was the light of men. The light shines in the dark-
ness, and the darkness has not overcome it.
—John 1:1-5 ESV

There is a disconcerting trend when it comes to the Bible, and it is reflected clearly in the direction of many of our churches and our nation in general. It is simply not read, and if it is, it is treated like a self-help book to be mended and shaped to our preferences and political affiliations. Preachers have softened its content in order to make God seem more "likable," "tolerant," and "inclusive." This has led us down a path that in many respects is even more dangerous than lack of Bible reading altogether. We have shaped an infallible and perfect word into our own image, and it shows.

We all read ourselves into the scripture to a degree. We are fallible human beings and the lens that we read the word in is certainly shaped by our experience and culture. We cannot be perfect in our interpretation, although we could use a huge amount of improvement.

In this chapter I want to show you how to take the word as it is, enjoy it, and live it out in a way that gives you access to the life and life more abundantly Jesus promises us in our submission to His will. This is the very first step in approaching the word correctly; we come to the word in submission to it, not in order to make it fit our perspective. The phrase is often used, "Let the Bible read you."

I got my very first Bible when I was 12 years old. My dad walked me into a Christian bookstore (they still existed when I was a pre-teen). I had no idea what I was choosing as far as translations are concerned or the world I was about to step into. I did know I liked leather and liked the smell of the pages. I ended up devouring it. I read the Bible from cover to cover at the age of 12 for the first time, in New American Standard. I certainly didn't understand every-thing I was reading, but it set a foundation in my life for consistent Bible reading that I am eternally grateful for.

I still read the Bible daily. I have to. I do not understand how a believer with complete access to a book that is thousands of years old, is absolutely true, and has all the answers required for life will not pick it up and simply start by reading. I'm not even mentioning proper study, just simply reading it and thinking deeply about what it is saying about who God is and how He should be worshiped. This book tells what the world is, what human beings are, and who *you* are and need to become. If you could simply answer those questions, wouldn't that make so many other answers fall into place?

Imagine having the actual power that formed the universe readily available to you. How did our world begin? With words. The weight of this truth is astounding in the very least. The study of language and words—indeed, how words create the cultures we live in—is at the very center of our world now. We have the words of life out of the mouth of Jesus. A whole book written by the inspiration of the Holy Spirit. Unassailable historically, theologically coherent, profound in its simple truth while displaying the dense complexity of humanity, the beginning and end of all literature, and powerful beyond what we can comprehend. The very word of the Emperor of the universe at our fingertips. How lightly we take it, and it shows.

> *For the word of God is living and active, sharper than any two-edged sword, piercing to the division of soul and of spirit, of joints and of marrow, and discerning the thoughts and intentions of the heart* (Hebrews 4:12 ESV).

So much of what we do in life is unimportant. I would suggest that we do not waste time taking in the word; we waste time when we don't. Imagine standing in the courts of heaven when your life is over and you are standing in the presence of the King. He asks you a few simple questions.

"Could you read?"

"Yes." (This is my assumption as these are words and you're reading them.)

"Did you have a Bible, did you have My word?"

"Yes."

"What did you do with it?"

"_____"

Enter your own answer thus far in your life. I am sure that, whether a person is a scholar with multiple PhDs or a layman with three different versions of the Bible lying around their home, neither will be able to answer the King that they had spent sufficient time reading and practicing the word. Of course we have to understand that it will never be "enough," but that there is always more.

We all have deep-seated questions that need answering, or at least a peace that the answer is in the hands of someone we trust.

Who is God and how do I worship Him?

What is this world we live in?

What are human beings?

Who am I?

Who do I need to become?

These are deep questions with answers only found in the person of God revealed in scripture. You cannot find the depth, profundity, simplicity, and tension of real practical wisdom for life anywhere else.

So where do you even start? Well, Genesis, the beginning, sets a brilliant stage for the unfolding of the rest of the biblical drama. It tells us that out of Spirit and the spoken word came life. It tells us that the Bible, from the start, is a book of the Spirit and the word—seemingly invisible things, but the two most valuable things to human meaning and modes of being.

You're Religious Anyway, Make Sure It's the Right One

For example, human beings simply do not live life without religion, without a form of worship. You can usually find your religion, or more appropriately your god, by seeing what you ask permission of on a daily basis to live. Anything that holds precedent over the call of Christ—whether it's work, or the gym, or friendships, or your kids—if you have to ask permission from that other thing in order to follow Jesus, and the answer more often than not determines your action, you've found yourself a god.

In the same way, you cannot go through life without communication. The spoken word, whether it plays in your head or comes out of your mouth, is the most powerful force in the human race. It builds up and tears down; it encourages and eviscerates. But for all the importance of the spoken word, we aren't exactly one hundred percent sure *why* it is so important. However, every single person is acutely aware of its power because they have felt it on the receiving and the giving ends. Whether you have been insulted or belittled or encouraged by a word, you understand its power over your life.

So we know from the outset of Genesis that the source of absolute truth and Spirit created the physical and spiritual universe that we live in.

My point—the Bible is a spiritual book, and the authors had a spiritual perspective and philosophy. In the West, we read it washed in materialism, but the material we see and experience in the world did not come first. God, who is Spirit, is pre-existent and eternal, is the "prime mover." This sets an important stage for the rest of what we read in scripture. The creator is, *ipso facto*, the owner of everything He makes.

So as we begin reading the Bible, we must see it as a book about how God, who is Spirit, is dealing within and through humanity for His glory. It is a spiritual book graciously given to us in a physical plane to show us reality as it truly exists.

We must come to terms with the fact that our experience is far from the whole picture, and our broken perception has the danger of removing truth from our perspective altogether.

The word of God is truth in a deeper sense than we can comprehend.

If the Bible is the fundamental basis for understanding reality as it truly is, how should we approach it in our sometimes sleepy quiet time on the couch?

Right here is where I will refuse to give you a Bible reading plan. The daily practice of reading, studying, and meditating on scripture is what you actually need. A plan can so often be a feel-good method of failing to actually be in the word. If you like to check boxes, though, have at it. In all seriousness, if that works for you there are 10 billion resources available for reading plans. But you should beware of shallow, half-hearted "devotionals" by celebrities that say more about the person writing them than the word itself. We all need to be taught the word, from the tiny toddling child to the triple doctorate in any field of theology. We are all trying to practice, to learn, this perfect word. Or, as C.S. Lewis cleverly suggested in his well-known fiction, take our "bent" way of thinking and make it straight.[1]

Before we jump into the actual practice of daily reading and study, I want to give some basic guidelines that will help you read scripture correctly.

How Should We Interpret the Bible?

First, get yourself a good translation of the Bible. I say translation because there are quite a few paraphrased versions of the Bible that are good for the market, but terrible for study and accuracy. The concern with many paraphrase versions is that the words are changed for emotional effect and do not accurately translate what the original author was trying to convey through the inspiration of the Holy Spirit. If God is writing a book, let's try and hear what He's saying the way He meant to say it. The word has already made its way through two languages to make its way to you. Make sure that when you are reading it in your native language it is a version that you can really trust. I like the English Standard Version and New International Version for study.

Second, the Bible can never mean what it never meant in the first place. This is a good starting point for reading and study because it leads to the correct questions regarding the passages you're meditating on and then applying to your daily life. We can so often read a passage and apply a metaphor to it that simply does not exist and wasn't meant by the original author.

Take, for example, the parable of the good Samaritan. How many times have you heard this preached and taught with every character representing someone in our daily lives, teaching us how to be kind or generous with our income? While all of these things may have their place in the overall narrative of scripture, this is not what Jesus was aiming at or how to interpret the parable.

The meaning of a parable is the parable itself—the whole story comes together in order to answer a question or make a particular point about the Kingdom Jesus is aiming at. Breaking up the parable into sections and making a point of a particular verse or a metaphor out of a section of the story is mostly bad practice.

Jesus was answering the lawyer's (the expert in the Mosaic Law's) question, which was, "Who is my neighbor?" The lawyer was trying to justify being a neighbor to some and not to others. Jesus used this story to answer the real question at hand and flipped it on its head. The real question, "Who was a good neighbor?" narrowed in on the personal responsibility of the lawyer. The crux of the parable was not an answer the original question asked. It was using a hated Samaritan as the shock to get attention for how you can be a good neighbor. Even the Samaritan knew that this man needed help and that setting aside laws of purity made sense when a human life was in peril.

So we can see that along with all the other parables, the whole thing is the metaphor; the entire narrative of the story makes a singular point. This is what makes parables memorable, even unforgettable. After all, that's what makes all the great stories great.

Remember, the Bible can never say what it has never said.[2] The intended meaning of the writer is the intended meaning of the Holy Spirit. The fancy word theologians use for how you interpret the scripture is *exegesis.*

Here is an example of poor exegesis that everyone who's been in a church for more than 30 seconds will have heard before. It's in the story of David. Many teachers and regular Bible-reading folks read the story of David and Goliath and think, "God wants me to conquer my giants and this is proof of that." In reality, the story is much deeper than that. It's a story of an intimidated people who did not have the actual resources to defeat a descendant of the Nephilim.[3] David—anointed, but not yet king (the *now* king but *not yet*)—killed him and cut off his head and led the people of Israel to victory, removing the stain from the land (see 1 Samuel 17).

The question we have to ask before we start declaring the promise of giant killing over our lives or ruminating on the meaning of the five smooth stones is, "What was the author trying to say?" He was telling a story of a savior of Israel—the early days of a savior of God's people. By the Holy Spirit, he was foreshadowing Christ, helping us long for a Savior in the midst of a battle that we simply cannot win against sin and death itself, the stain of humanity. In this regard, we cannot slay the real giants that affect our daily lives—the bad habits, the habitual sin, the anger, the lust. Fortunately, the anointed King, Jesus, can.

The Bible needs to mean what it originally meant at the time of writing before it begins to unfold before us as a book for our daily lives. Start here. Then watch your whole world change.

Third, who was this written for, by whom, and in what context? To gain a fuller and deeper understanding of the word we must, to the best of our ability, understand these concepts. Take the often quarreled over "women in ministry and preaching" question. No matter what side of the debate you land on, you had better know why Paul the apostle was writing this letter to the Corinthians, what the context was, and *then* we can begin to apply this to *our* current context.

Fourth, let the Bible interpret itself. If you are really struggling with a passage of scripture, look at the edges of your Bible or the footnotes and you can clearly see where that scripture is cross-referenced. You can also just go online and look it up. A world of interpretation is at your fingertips, but use caution when it comes to commentaries and blogs. Your best bet is to find related scripture and add it together in a journal to create a kind of "recipe" for biblical interpretation.[4]

So sit down and put a journal next to you, maybe two, and here is what I recommend you do.

Put one journal down in front of you for distraction—I'll explain that in just a moment.

Put one journal down in front of you that is for questions and thoughts regarding the word you are reading and meditating on.

As you read through the Bible, *you must realize that it is not about you. It is about God.* This is a relief to me. Why? Because we couldn't carry the weight of the story. We sabotaged it in the first few chapters, then God began His redemptive work that culminates in Christ, the Redeemer Himself.

Once you have begun to read this way, it's a good starting place to meditate on scripture. That word, *meditation,* has been hijacked by new agers and "spiritual people" in the West. There is a remarkable difference between biblical meditation and eastern mystic-style meditation.

The eastern mystics and all their derivatives attempt to empty themselves of all thought, to go blank. This is, from a spiritual perspective, a great opportunity for demonic powers to place their own thoughts on that blank page of their minds.

Biblical meditation, on the other hand, is to fill yourself with the word of God. Paul says in Philippians 4:8 (ESV):

> *Finally, brothers, whatever is true, whatever is honorable, whatever is just, whatever is pure,*

whatever is lovely, whatever is commendable, if there is any excellence, if there is anything worthy of praise, think about these things.

And again in 2 Timothy 3:16-17 (ESV):

All Scripture is breathed out by God and profitable for teaching, for reproof, for correction, and for training in righteousness, that the man of God may be complete, equipped for every good work.

In Joshua, we are commanded to meditate on scripture:

This Book of the Law shall not depart from your mouth, but you shall meditate on it day and night, so that you may be careful to do according to all that is written in it. For then you will make your way prosperous, and then you will have good success (Joshua 1:8 ESV).

So how do you do that? The way I got started was simply reading a passage, reading it again, then reading it out loud and finding ways to carry it with me beyond my secret place to let it wash over me all day long (notecards and phone reminders, etc.). You are constantly eating spiritual meat and bread when you are aiming your thoughts at scripture.

Many Christians come to us for prayer because they feel they are in a dry spiritual season. In many cases, they are simply bored and not truly *searching* the scriptures for their spiritual sustenance from God. They want the word to tell them something that will make them feel better. This is not always the case—the word of God won't be bartered with or manipulated to fit you. You were created to take the shape of the word, and not vice versa. Then you will have real satisfaction, not just fleeting happiness.

Let the word of God be your comfort, your supply, and your strength. When things are good, you've got the word. When things are hell on earth, you've got the word. When you are in cruise control, you've got the word to snap you out of it. Hear what I am trying to say—spiritually dry places are where demons go when they are cast out, not the children of God. There is always as much food at the table as you want to eat. Cut out the donuts; eat the meat. It's life to your bones and a river of living water that will flow out of you.

Learn to meditate. Practice meditation. But not in the idiotic way the world teaches. You must be filled with the word of God to fulfill your calling. No prophetic word or good message from a pulpit will fill this void.

To conclude, the last and often forgotten portion that provides the real power on your path to being victorious is to simply *do what the Bible says.*

> *Everyone then who hears these words of mine and does them will be like a wise man who built his house on the rock. And the rain fell, and the floods came, and the winds blew and beat on that house, but it did not fall, because it had been founded on the rock. And everyone who hears these words of mine and does not do them will be like a foolish man who built his house on the sand. And the rain fell, and the floods came, and the winds blew*

*and beat against that house, and it fell, and great
was the fall of it* (Matthew 7:24-27 ESV).

Jesus says that the commandment of His Father leads
to eternal life.

*I know that his command leads to eternal life. So
whatever I say is just what the Father has told me
to say* (John 12:50 NIV).

The implications of this are almost too expansive to
comprehend. Jesus the Son of God submits Himself to the
Father and obeys His commands. What this tells us is that
much of the power of scripture is in acting upon it. This
is where I want to dissuade you from locking yourself in a
closet for eternity and just thinking about the word. It is
the command to go and do that really cements the word
of God into our hearts.

The Jesus Method of Teaching

"Tell me and I forget; teach me and I may
remember; involve me and I learn."
                                   —20th-century maxim

Jesus' method of teaching the word was far more like
show and tell as opposed to memorizing information and
jotting it down on a test. The test of whether or not you
truly know the word of God—and see it for what it truly
is—is real-world application. I often wondered if passages
like the Sermon on the Mount (the end of which is mentioned Matthew 7:24-27) were actually possible to really
do in my life. Could I actually be like Jesus? Be obedient

to the word? Get rid of my anger and lust that were constantly crouching like roaring lions to devour me? Truly, for a long time I just did not. I made myself feel better by thinking that God's grace would smooth it all over in the end. However, as I continued to read scripture, especially the words and deeds of Jesus and Paul the apostle, my angst and dissatisfaction became overwhelming. It was time to be honest with myself, as perhaps you need to as well, that I just wasn't doing what Jesus asked me to do and I didn't really know how. This is where a genuine look at the word of God led me, and I hope after this chapter you are dissatisfied as well. We are commanded to obey, but how?

Lots of practice, lots of imperfect forward movement, but forward nonetheless. The phrase is often uttered, "It's not so simple." It *is* simple, just difficult. What is more difficult in the end is answering to Jesus and being salted with fire on your way into heaven. Decide that you want your full reward in this life and the next and begin to realize that the real life you are looking for is in doing what Jesus tells you to do. This is what real freedom looks like.

Again you may be asking, "But how?" Well, you're in luck—that is exactly what this book is for and why I wrote it for you. Practicing spiritual disciplines does not just make you a practitioner of a self-soothing new form of religiosity. When we aim for communion with Christ and obedience to Him in our practice, we become the *type of person* who behaves like Jesus.

Keep in mind that the aim is not simply adherence when it comes to reading the word—as beneficial for some as that may be. The goal here is what is called sanctification, or a transformation into the image and likeness of Jesus through the power of the Holy Spirit, working and practicing these new disciplines you are learning.

Remember to simply stay on the path, and that path is always leading up and toward Jesus the person, not Jesus the idea.

The Path

The word of God in simple practice. First, set a pattern within your secret place for reading and meditating on the word. Then in your secret place, go through these steps with a favorite or difficult passage of scripture.

1. Get a good translation.

Make sure you have a translation and not a paraphrase for your time in serious study and meditation.

2. The Bible cannot mean what it never meant.

What was the original author's intent and meaning? What the author means, the Holy Spirit means.

3. Who was this written for, by whom, and in what context?

Look these up for this passage with whatever resources you have.

4. Let the Bible interpret itself.

Write down the passages that relate to this one and let it fill out the entire biblical perspective.

_____

_____

_____

_____

_____

_____

_____

_____

_____

_____

_____

_____

_____

_____

5. *Do what it says.*

Share with a spouse, mentor, or friend what you will be doing to obey the word, then do it daily. It could be showing secret acts of kindness, praying for someone you hate every day, working out instead of watching pornography, asking for a pause to collect yourself in an argument with a loved one, and responding with kindness.

Notes

1. This word is consistently used in C.S. Lewis' space trilogy to describe thoughts and actions that stray away from God's intended purpose.

2. "A text cannot mean what it could never have meant for its original readers/hearers." (Gordon D. Fee, *How to Read the Bible for All It's Worth* [Grand Rapids, MI: Zondervan, 2014], 34.)

3. Evil spiritual beings that procreated and had descendants that were actively shedding blood and helped usher in the Noahic flood.

4. For further instruction on how to read the Bible really well and begin to see it open up to you, pick up two books from which I draw much of the information in this chapter: *The Unseen Realm* by Dr. Michael S. Heiser and *How to Read the Bible for All its Worth* by Gordon D. Fee.

Chapter 7

EFFECTIVE PRAYER

We pray feebly because we live feebly.
—E.M. Bounds, *The Necessity of Prayer*

A lack of fervency in prayer shows your true desire. When you lack passionate, consistent, prayer it is because it is not the presence of God you long for or even the thing prayed for, but a wish and a want for a transaction that fulfills a temporary inadequacy in you. We so often pray weak and, bluntly speaking, boring prayers because our dreams and desires are our own and not God's.

Personally, I hate most corporate prayer gatherings. They tend toward unspecific, long, aimless, and lukewarm prayers that achieve no purpose but our feeling good about having a prayer meeting. Well, perhaps by God's grace something does get done. I will not dare take that from Him. He hears the groanings of our hearts, after all.

> *Likewise the Spirit helps us in our weakness. For we do not know what to pray for as we ought, but the Spirit himself intercedes for us with groanings too deep for words* (Romans 8:26 ESV).

The Heart of Prayer

But is there groaning in our hearts? Do we desire the will of God and His Kingdom come with such a deep and burning passion that it *becomes* something almost completely unutterable?

Do you lose sleep over it?

Do lost souls haunt your secret place of prayer?

Does the dream placed in your heart by the Holy Spirit make you burn?

Have you burned the ships so there is no return?

Is your plan B in the trash heap where it belongs?

Or do you pray for the pots of stew and onions like you had in your former life in Egypt?

> *Now the rabble that was among them had a strong craving. And the people of Israel also wept again and said, "Oh that we had meat to eat! We remember the fish we ate in Egypt that cost nothing, the cucumbers, the melons, the leeks, the onions, and the garlic"* (Numbers 11:4-5 ESV).

Do you conjure your own small dreams that stir no passion?

Consistently filling your prayer life with petitions for temporary things will leave you longing for more. Perhaps, even if the thing is received, it will lead you to quit prayer altogether.

We need a revival of personal and corporate prayer in which the desires of God and His presence are the whole list. For doesn't He already know what you need? Jesus specifically told us not to babble on like the pagans and repeat ourselves.

Imagine it like this. Let's say your rent needs to get paid this week. So naturally, you take the direct approach and pray for a miracle to see that money come in. Perhaps it does, and praise God for taking care of His children. However, perhaps there is a better way.

The old adage, "Teach a man to fish and you've fed him for a lifetime" applies well here. In the example of the rent, God has given you a fish out of mercy. The alternative, the prayer of faith, can produce far more. This is the currency of the Kingdom of Heaven! *Faith!* I want to shift your mindset and your heart from praying to get by or for another short-sighted miracle. We need to aim for the Kingdom of Heaven invading our lives. To pray prayers that actually stir our passion to seek the Lord for real breakthrough. I want to teach you how to fish with a net. It's simple, although at first awkward and difficult to do. So here we go.

Listen When the King Is Present

Step number one: Just shut up. And listen.

Take the very first portion of your prayer, in the presence of the Emperor of the universe, and do what is appropriate. Listen to Him! Do not begin to speak unless you are spoken to. His presence is promised by Christ Himself, as soon as you shut that door and set aside the time for Him.

> But when you pray, go into your room and shut
> the door and pray to your Father who is in secret.
> And your Father who sees in secret will reward you
> (Matthew 6:6 ESV).

When you hear from the Lord, write it down first, whatever comes to your spirit. Then you can check with scripture and begin to truly learn the voice of the Lord.

We must understand that His dreams for us are far better than the dreams we create for ourselves in the flesh. Why? Because He *knows you*. Your Father in heaven loves you and it is His *good pleasure* to give you the Kingdom.

> So don't be afraid, little flock. For it gives your
> Father great happiness to give you the Kingdom
> (Luke 12:32 NLT).

God's Plan Is Better Than Yours

Trust is the paramount value for stewarding your prayer life. Submitting your plans to the Lord does not mean telling God what you feel like doing and asking Him to bless it. What if He is a good Father after all and those plans would end up destroying you? Or you would end up hating the outcome and not feeling like you had meaningful work?

Or it overwhelms you and you do a poor job of raising your children and loving your spouse?

I am not saying that every idea you have is out of the flesh and going to blow up your life. What I am saying is that the God of heaven and earth has plans for you that are far beyond your imagination. As well as the fact that when He speaks, He creates. Imagine this—the Creator of the universe actually *creating* something in your spirit by speaking to you in your secret place.

This is the best kept secret of effective prayer—listening and then responding to what is already on the Lord's heart for you. We so often come with petitions that are immediate and desperate when we could be praying for something far larger, far better, that would solve our immediate and desperate prayer request. Take the time to listen.

Every single person on earth loves to be listened to and given attention. God is in many ways the same. Even understanding our distractions and frailty, God likes to come where He is welcome.

When you are listening and God is speaking life-giving words to you, keep them and treasure them. Then ask Him, and keep in mind this is not a formula but a starting point, "God, what is on Your heart, what can I pray for, what is Your will?"

Imagine praying the dreams of the Almighty God, the Lord of Hosts, the Maker of Heaven and earth.

Would this change your life? Certainly. Do you think your rent would get taken care of—or that you would even care? This is fishing with a net. We beg at the shore for a handout from the Master's table when He invites us into the deep places in His heart to accomplish His perfect will on the earth. Along the way, your little list of orphan desires will get swallowed up in Him, and that list will both change and be provided for.

I am *not* saying your desires don't matter to God—quite the opposite. Your desires matter to Him far more than they matter to you. The real issue we run into is, in the light of eternity, do we even know what we really want? I am often plagued by this question myself, even in the midst of the most powerful ministry I've seen so far in my life. Literally thousands are being baptized, awakening is breaking out among God's people, the lost are coming home in the thousands. I always tend to look again, no matter how good things seem or the affirmation I receive; I take my gaze and focus on my Father in heaven and I ask Him, "Is this what You want?"

This is why it is so important that we neither flag nor fail to pray and practice being silent before God. We *must* hear His will. It is not optional for the life of a disciple, for it wasn't optional in the life of God in the flesh, Jesus Himself.

In the midst of failure God's voice is simple and easy to hear, and prayer seems to pour out of us like an unstoppable mountain stream. When things are good, we all tend toward thinking we've done it, we've arrived, and our perceived need tends to diminish. The truth of the matter is that we need God far more in what the world, or most ministries, would call success. At the peak of His popularity, Jesus got away so as not to be made king of Israel. A man who fed five thousand with a few loaves of bread and a handful of fish certainly seemed like the right candidate to remove the Romans and establish the Kingdom right now. But what did He do? Left. Got alone. Prayed.

If Jesus needed this, then so do we.

Now you know why.

How, then, can we take what we have heard and effectively petition God? Would it not be far better if prayer actually worked? If you saw the results of prevailing prayer in your life, wouldn't that drive you to pray even more?

Your next practice for effective fervent prayer is praying the word of God.

> *For the word of God is living and active, sharper than any two-edged sword, piercing to the division of soul and of spirit, of joints and of marrow, and discerning the thoughts and intentions of the heart* (Hebrews 4:12 ESV).

When we pray the word of God, we put something living into motion on our behalf. God is not separate from His word and it never "returns void." This means that when you are praying the word, you are praying the thoughts and intentions of God, which never fail.

Again, trust and faith are the key ingredients to an effective prayer life. As you begin to build your relationship with God in the secret place every single day, you will begin to see that nobody can be trusted more than Him.

This will give you the confidence you need in prayer to "push through."

As you pray from the psalms or from promises in the Bible, you will begin to be transformed yourself. Many times our prayers aren't answered because we are not yet the type of people who can actually receive them. God doesn't give out candy to a diabetic child. We first need to understand that prayer in large part transforms us into tools God can actually use and trust with His dreams. The word will do just that.

Practice praying in and from the word and watch what God does.

Last, and perhaps the best of all, Jesus directly tells us how to pray in the gospels. You can find this in Matthew 6:9-14, but I will break it down for you here to give you a form for prayer. When you practice this, it will teach you to pray like Jesus.

> *Pray like this: "Our Father in heaven, hallowed be your name"* (Matthew 6:9 ESV).

Let's remember as we go through this prayer that these are the words of God telling us how to pray. It will help your prayer life take shape. Just like playing a musical instrument, you will at first feel awkward and halting playing scales; then you can start to *really play*.

The first thing Jesus teaches us to do in prayer is to put God in His proper place. This, in turn, places us properly in the family of God, addressing the supreme Head of our family with respect and honor. We enter His gates with thanksgiving or praise and worship to the King. The first thing that you do in prayer is worship God, say what you are thankful for, praise His name! This will set the tone for the rest of your prayer—placing God in His proper place in your heart.

> *Your kingdom come, your will be done, on earth*
> *as it is in heaven* (Matthew 6:10 ESV).

This is where listening and praying what is on the Father's heart is vital. We are praying that His complete will is done in and through our lives as we pray. If we know His will and we can pray for His will, we will see the Kingdom effectively expanded in our lives and the lives of those around us. We want God's will to be perfectly executed on the earth, so we pray for more of His Kingdom to come by the power of His Holy Spirit.

> *Give us this day our daily bread* (Matthew 6:11 ESV).

Now after we have worshiped and placed God above ourselves and our circumstances and then prayed for His will and His Kingdom to come, we address our daily needs. God deeply cares about us, and we realize this more as we continue to practice prayer. Lay out your needs and desires before God, share your heart with Him completely, give control of tomorrow over to Him.

Notice how it says "give us *this day* our daily bread." Jesus is clear that worrying in the Kingdom is actually a sin! We are not to be concerned with how tomorrow will turn out. This doesn't negate planning or good stewardship, but it does remind us that when it comes down to it you are only in control of a very small portion of what happens in life. What we can do is pray and petition God, who truly is in control, to work on our behalf.

My wife and I have lived for months at a time when we could not pay rent, and we have lived in abundance when we have not had to worry about money. (Don't worry, there's a whole chapter coming on that.) In either circumstance, I have learned that worry is a huge waste of energy and especially time, which just so happens to be your most valuable resource by far. So manage what you can manage, and bring it all before your Father in heaven. Let Him be sovereign even over your daily needs. You will find in the end that Jesus is the bread you are really looking for and your needs will get met, especially with an attitude of abundance, gratitude, and generosity.

> *And forgive us our debts, as we also have forgiven our debtors* (Matthew 6:12 ESV).

A strong assumption is made here by Jesus that we will be people who do not hold a grudge. You have racked up incalculable debts that you owe to God. The slightest sin against the highest authority deserves the judgment of God and hell itself. But you were given your freedom; you were bought with a price. So forgiveness, which may come more naturally to some than to others, should be a daily practice.

Think through those who have offended you and pray for them. Think about financial debts that you can forgive. Let go of whatever your parents did that you still carry around and lay them before your Father. Why? Don't they owe you? Take a look at what Jesus has to say about that.

> *But if you do not forgive others their trespasses, neither will your Father forgive your trespasses* (Matthew 6:15 ESV).

This is His statement right at the end of this prayer. Forgiveness needs to be practiced; it's a muscle that doesn't come naturally. Everyone demands some level of justice, and they will receive justice in the end. In most circumstances that aren't life threatening, leave the justice up to God and you'll set yourself free from the poison of bitterness. We must start from the place where we are given even our breath by God Himself, and He holds life and death in His hands. We are fortunate to have another day on earth to pray.

Forgive, and it will be forgiven. Make sure your measure of forgiveness is large—you may need it in return someday.

> *And lead us not into temptation, but deliver us from evil* (Matthew 6:13 ESV).

Temptation is not something we should willingly seek to strengthen ourselves. This is the height of folly. We simply do not have the moral courage in most cases to consistently face it and overcome it, especially if we make allowances for ourselves to seek it out. Boundaries, parameters, disciplines all make this a lot simpler. If you don't want to get fat, get the ice cream out of the freezer and throw it away. Then you simply don't have to work up the moral courage and grit every time you walk by to say no to a delicious pint of two thousand calories. We often don't have what it takes, and that's okay if we are aware of it. If we are not, we think we are standing when we are truly ready to fall in our pride. So ask for help!

This is what Jesus is getting at—that if at all possible we would be guarded from temptation by the Holy Spirit. That we would be led away from it in order to live a holy life. I personally hate being tempted and hate sin; so does God. He does not want you to be tempted beyond your ability to resist. So ask that He keep you from it every day. You might find that this works on a number of levels in your life.

I pray (yes, actually pray) that this chapter has stirred up a passion in you to pray not just more, but effectively. You can actually pray and continue to learn how to do so. I know that with so many distractions, with work and kids and bills on the brain, it can seem like just getting started is a waste of time. Remember that no time spent in the presence of God, being with Him and petitioning Him, is ever a waste.

It was prayer that began all great revivals.

It was prayer that brought down and lifted up empires.

It was prayer that Jesus leaned on in the most difficult moment of His life before His suffering.

We should be a praying people. Not just because we should, but because we serve a living God and prayer works.

The Path

Write down the Lord's Prayer in your journal (Matthew 6:9-14), and for one week use it in your secret place as a guide to your prayers.

Worship

> *Pray like this: "Our Father in heaven, hallowed be*
> *your name"* (Matthew 6:9 ESV).

Start out your prayer time with placing God in His rightful place. Lay everything else aside and worship Him with prayers of thanksgiving and with worship music playing (that doesn't talk about you, but about Him). The point here is to genuinely worship God from your heart to begin prayer.

> *Your kingdom come, your will be done, on earth*
> *as it is in heaven* (Matthew 6:10 ESV).

Next we petition God to bring His Kingdom to this earth in a way that earth looks like heaven. We ask that what He wants to get done, both in the world and in our personal lives, would be done without exception. We are centering ourselves on the will of God revealed through His word.

> *Give us this day our daily bread* (Matthew 6:11
> ESV).

What is it that you need? Your Father in heaven already knows what your needs are, but now that He has been exalted above your issues and needs and you have asked for His will to be done, your heart is in the proper place to ask for what you really need. Lay it all before Him and see what He does with your needs.

> *And forgive us our debts, as we also have forgiven*
> *our debtors* (Matthew 6:12 ESV).

This is a two-part prayer. First, we ask that God forgive us, and at the same time we forgive those who owe us. Whether it be justice or money, we place all justice in the hands of a just God and release our own mistakes and those of others into His more than capable hands. Forgive.

> *And lead us not into temptation, but deliver us from evil* (Matthew 6:13 ESV).

Temptation is brutal. Ask that God remove it from you in all cases, to purify your heart to a degree where the things that used to tempt you no longer do. Ask for deliverance from the work of the devil and those under his power, whether you are aware of it or not. This is spiritual warfare—first letting God into your personal struggle in order to be victorious, and then praying for others that they may be delivered from the same. Keep a list of people you are blessing in this way and see what God does in their lives.

Chapter 8

SPIRITUAL BREAD

Bear up the hands that hang down; by faith and prayer support the tottering knee; reprove, encourage. Have you appointed any days of fasting and prayer? Storm the throne of grace, and persevere therein, and mercy will come down.
—JOHN WESLEY, letter to his
sister, March 1, 1774

At the beginning of this year I completed my first ever 40-day fast. I felt the impression that it was coming soon, that I needed to get ready for it. I knew that this year (2022) was going to be beyond what I imagined in favor, success, and difficulty. I needed to be as close to Jesus as possible, to be able to smell the sweat on Him as we climbed the mountain of prayer together.

So on January 1 it started. I had done 21 days before; I'd done multiple 10-day and 3-day fasts before. But something felt different about this, and let me tell you, it was a fight. The food wasn't really the issue, even though cooking for family and little ones can be somewhat of a struggle when you haven't eaten for three weeks. Chicken nuggets start to look like the best meal of your life pretty quickly into a genuine water fast.

Death of the Flesh, Death of Self

The real struggle was my flesh dying. I was constantly tired after 20 or so days in. I tried to work and carry on as normal, but something shifted and I just could not do anything in a completely normal fashion. This hit me far deeper than expected. Being weak, dependent on help, and really of no physical use to anyone hit the core of my pride.

I picked up my phone and called my mentor Ed Pioreck, who wrote a book, *The Father Loves You,* that had a deep and lasting impact on my life. Well, he and his wife praying for me and then weeping in his living room really was the start; I picked up the book after I experienced it. I asked him how this whole long fast "worked." After all, I had responsibilities. I had a wife and three small children—what should I do? He then said something I will be eternally grateful for and pass on to every generation in my family: "Parker, remember that the fast *is* the work. Your 'job' is to be near to Jesus." I realized then that my flesh dying was precious to Jesus, that He really just wanted me. At this point, that is about all I could do—just be with Him. The last 10 days of the fast, I was down almost 40 pounds and very weak. So every morning, I just woke up, turned my fire on in the living room, sat in my leather chair, and read the Bible until I fell asleep.

When it comes to how a fast "works," it needs to be absolutely clear to you that it really isn't the work at all. It is the dying of the flesh so you can be near to Jesus that is the aim of every fast. Like what was mentioned in the chapters before this—all biblical spiritual practice is designed to bring you near to Jesus and make you the type of person who is willingly and joyfully obedient to Him. The work of a fast is being with Him—that is where the transformation really takes place. In this case, there is literally less of you and more of Him.

I can't describe it completely in our limited language, but this fast broke me in the best possible way. I had my list of things I was fasting for, my visions and dreams, my hopes, my desires. In the end, none of them mattered; it was just Him. I only wanted Jesus, and I could tangibly feel His desire for me. Everything stripped bare, I was naked and weak before Him. The "work" didn't get done, but I was completely undone, and that's what He wanted.

Fasting is a key to the Almighty's heart. I won't give you a false idea here—it's not easy, but that's kind of the point. If you can, say, not eat for multiple days or multiple weeks, in what other ways will crucifying your flesh seem so much easier? Your body needs food in the end, but your corrupted flesh does not need so many things.

To be clear here, I am not saying your body is evil, and that is never what is intended with the use of the word *flesh*. What I mean is "flesh" as Paul the apostle meant it—the things that war against your submission to the Holy Spirit. I *do not* mean your body. God actually loves your body as His temple, and caring for it should be a top priority in our lives. Desires of the flesh are embedded in your body and in your heart.

> *It is not what goes into the mouth that defiles a person, but what comes out of the mouth; this defiles a person* (Matthew 15:11 ESV).

And:

> *The good person out of the good treasure of his heart produces good, and the evil person out of his evil treasure produces evil, for out of the abundance of the heart his mouth speaks* (Luke 6:45 ESV).

Fasting replaces the false treasures of this world with the King Himself. Then, what fruit you produce becomes far more oriented to the desires of heaven than what you perhaps even thought you wanted at the beginning of your fast.

Imagine right now something in your life you have been trying to quit, especially something that if you gave it up would lead you into a more holy life. A habit or sin that, if removed, would mean you could shed shame and be nearer to Jesus every single day. Now I want to suggest something. Take an indirect approach—fast.

It's a simple fact that you *cannot* get rid of a terrible habit by simply focusing on getting rid of it. You can't stop being angry by just trying to stop being angry. You cannot stop watching porn by focusing on stopping. You cannot stop fantasizing by focusing on quitting your daydreaming. You have to take the indirect approach and create a positive habit and the fortitude to stick with it. You have to replace your evil desires with good or you will be worse off, more ashamed, and more destitute spiritually than before. Fasting clears out the dead wood. All that is not bearing fruit in your life. In all the time that you would spend eating meals, you're allowing the Holy Spirit to work on you.

> *Now there were in the church at Antioch prophets and teachers, Barnabas, Simeon who was called Niger, Lucius of Cyrene, Manaen a lifelong friend of Herod the tetrarch, and Saul. While they were worshiping the Lord and fasting, the Holy Spirit said, "Set apart for me Barnabas and Saul for the work to which I have called them." Then after fasting and praying they laid their hands on them and sent them off* (Acts 13:1-3 ESV).

Every Christian should fast. Fasting is the single most brutal hammer in your arsenal in the war against the "flesh." This is not a Christian weight loss strategy or a trinket in your tool box of things you've done for Jesus. Fasting teaches you to be like Jesus. Your sense of His presence and the word with you will be heightened, praying becomes more natural, and it teaches you a discipline that practiced in the physical has a spiritual result.

Like I have said, Jesus cares about your body. In fact, He is resurrected in a physical body right now seated at the right hand of the Father. It matters that you offer your body to God as a living sacrifice. There is a reason that we lift our hands when we worship, there is a reason we use our voices to sing and pray, there is a reason and a time to be on our knees in the presence of God, there is a reason for tears of repentance and tears of joy in God's presence. It matters that Jesus' body hung on a cross, was resurrected, ascended, and is returning in glory—all of this in a body. Jesus fasted in His body.

> *And when you fast, do not look gloomy like the hypocrites, for they disfigure their faces that their fasting may be seen by others. Truly, I say to you, they have received their reward* (Matthew 6:16 ESV).

When you fast, not *if* you fast. Jesus spent 40 days in the wilderness, as a perfect Man, before He began His public ministry. I cannot stress enough the importance of fasting as a regular part of the believer's life and the life of the church. So many people want the results of fasting and prayer without stepping into it. They want the secret. What can I do without it being so hard? In the end, the difficulty is not the point; it really is who you become and your nearness to Jesus. Those who are close to Him, He can trust with His directives. They know His heart.

If you are having trouble hearing God clearly, if you are looking for direction, looking for breakthrough, contending for revival or for a deeply lost loved one—lay your body down on the altar of sacrifice and fast, and fire will come down. It may not be exactly what you expected, but I promise you that it will be worth it.

The Path

Choose a date and start a fast with a friend, spouse, or discipleship group. If your church does a yearly fast and it's close at hand, do a true fast with your church. What I don't mean is giving up a regular vice such as social media, TV, alcohol, or any regular habit. When I define *fast* in this book, it is directly related to the refusal to eat food.

Remember that the work of a fast is to be with Jesus.

Purchase a journal specifically for this fast or mark a spot in your journal where you begin fasting and write in it every day. Write down two to three things you're praying for breakthrough in. Remember that your desires may change and should change during your fast. I've often found my desires fall to the side of my desire for Jesus. When that comes, don't resist it; let that be your focus.

Have a reading plan in your Bible or a particular book you are diving into. If it's your first time going through a fast, I highly recommend one of the gospels, Romans, or Ephesians. Stay in that book the whole time and let it become your meditation. This doesn't mean you can't read other parts of the Bible—just focus on your chosen plan or book.

That's it—you know what to do. Finish this fast and you won't regret it.

Chapter 9

ALONE

*A certain brother went to Abbot Moses in
Scete, and asked him for a good word. And
the elder said to him: Go, sit in your cell,
and your cell will teach you everything.*
—THOMAS MERTON, *The Wisdom of the Desert*

Being alone is terrifying to most people. Our society is
filled with constant noise to the point where even if we
do find a place to get quiet, the echoes of that noise continually reverberate through our brain like a constant
dripping of water while we are trying to fall asleep. Noise,
the constant noise.

I am not just talking about external noise. This can be avoided by simply finding a naturally quiet space, moving or vacationing out of a city, or locking yourself in a white padded room. Yet like our friend who finds himself in a room with no sharp objects and pillows for walls, the noise will follow you in your own heart.

You see, the biblical perspective on the mind is different from our perfectly divided Greek tripartite being, usually described as body, soul, and spirit. What we fail to recognize when we divide the parts of ourselves into neat little sections is that they all affect one another. When the Bible uses the word *heart*, it is talking about the governing, decision-making will of a human being. Think about it this way. When Solomon says in Proverbs 4:23 (NCB), "*Guard your heart with all possible vigilance, for from it flow the wellsprings of life,*" he's not just saying be careful about your "feelings"; he's reminding us that we need to be watchful over the direction of our deepest thoughts. For these thoughts produce what we see in our life. This is the heart, your very center.

Think about all the greatest decisions you've made in your life, the most uplifting and soaring experiences, as well as the seasons of life that drag you through the valley of the shadow of death. What was it that made these experiences what they are? What part of you was making the decisions to arrive there? I guarantee you it wasn't purely the frontal lobe of your brain making one logical decision after another. Most of the greatest disappointments and greatest achievements in our lives begin with a leap of faith.

- Marriage
- Children
- Salvation
- Moving into the unknown
- Pioneering a new work

These decisions happen in the human heart.

Here, I am laying the groundwork for a human experience in God that very few ever approach. For if you find yourself in the midst of chaos and your heart is quiet and attentive to the King of the universe, no situation presents itself as disastrous or completely overwhelming.

The truth is that you have no idea how loud life is until you find a place to be quiet. This is truly the place where you will learn to deal with yourself in the presence of Almighty God. It is terrifying and exhilarating. You will see how your heart and mind scream for true peace. With the distractions of entertainment and numbing agents like alcohol and social media gone, all that is left is you and the God of the universe. This is where the work begins.

Silence gets to the "heart" of the matter, and if we can quiet down and listen, words of creation and hope will be spoken to us from the counsel of heaven. Right here, in this place where you are undistracted and focused on baring your heart before God and just listening, is where greatness in the Kingdom of Heaven is truly made.

> *Be still, and know that I am God. I will be exalted among the nations, I will be exalted in the earth!*
> (Psalm 46:10 ESV)

When we are still and our heart knows that it knows that God is truly who He says He is, He will be exalted first in our hearts and then the wide world around us.

How is this even possible? You have a lot to do, a flood of responsibility. You have your marriage (or lack thereof), kids, job, work, church, friends, household tasks, the dreams, the side hustle, food to eat, time to work out, hobbies, bills to pay, bills to catch up on, etc. It all creates an overwhelming swirl that can leave us desperate for peace and not sure how to achieve it.

The first thing you need to realize is that this is a gift. The new age garbage about finding yourself, self-actualization, manifestation, personality tests, achieving your personal dreams—all of it is garbage. Without God, all of these things end up simply causing you to slip into secular humanism that will leave you emptier and without peace or hope. Jesus said this to His disciples:

> *Peace I leave with you; my peace I give to you. Not as the world gives do I give to you. Let not your hearts be troubled, neither let them be afraid* (John 14:27 ESV).

Jesus leaves us peace, but not as the world offers it. No amount of money, knowledge, achievement, status, or spiritual "ascent" we see so often in Christian circles will give you peace. Only Jesus can do that.

So how do we receive this gift? The key is in verse 26 that occurs just before this. *"But the Helper, the Holy Spirit, whom the Father will send in my name, he will teach you all things and bring to your remembrance all that I have said to you*" (John 14:26 ESV). The Holy Spirit comes as a Helper, and how does He help? By reminding us of everything Jesus has said and done. The key to real peace is the indwelling Holy Spirit who reminds us of Jesus, His words, and His finished work.

The unavoidable result of the discipline of silence is the realization that you are indeed a mess, just like everyone else. The joy-filled outcome of the discipline of silence is that when you let the Holy Spirit truly take over, you are reminded of Jesus and all that He has said and done for you. So take a deep breath, because as you peer into the darkness you will see a great light, and the darkness cannot overcome it.

> *In the beginning was the Word, and the Word was with God, and the Word was God. He was in the beginning with God. All things were made through him, and without him was not any thing made that was made. In him was life, and the life was the light of men. The light shines in the darkness, and the darkness has not overcome it* (John 1:1-5 ESV).

Silence Is Not Navel Gazing

The point of silence is not to navel gaze and tinker with your inner self. This won't work and is the world's way of finding peace, which as you can plainly see is failing miserably in a circus of chaos. The central purpose of silence is to hear from the Lord. To hear the word of God so that you may have peace. After all, what are the chaos and self-destructive patterns in our life a result of? Lack of peace, of course, but that lack of peace comes from our trying to build a foundation in our lives with our own works and achievements and not the word of God.

When God spoke, the universe was made. When He speaks into your heart, that same word builds a foundation in you that you can build on. His word is life eternal. When you separate yourself from trying to bite and scratch and claw your way to build something on this earth and can listen to the eternal word of God, you can build your house, your life, on the rock.

Alright, so now you know the point is listening and hearing the word, not just being quiet. So where to start?

This is so simple that it hurts, but very few will actually dive into this space.

First, set aside time on your calendar. Whether it is a retreat away from the regular duties of life or an early hour in the morning while your home is still quiet. Set an actual time to practice this.

I first learned how to be silent by going to silent places. The noise in my heart was so unbelievably loud that it took days to quiet it down. Pick a place on a map—whether you're a hotel person or a tent person, it doesn't matter. Just find a place where you can be still and not have responsibilities for this time. The sacrifice really matters. You have to lay down the time, your most valuable resource, to hear God. The retreat model is a good starting point because you are in the process of learning how to do this. Get away; shut off your tech. I promise you, whoever you are, that the world will not fall apart in your absence. The world has a way of doing that whether you are present or not, so take the time.

When you get away, I recommend that you fast. This clarifies your purpose and is an added discipline that continues to kill off the flesh.

Second, have a distinct purpose. What do you want to hear from God? What needs to be sorted out? What struggles are you facing? What needs answers or, better said, what situations in your life do you need God to show up in? As you practice being silent and hearing from Him, you will realize that you won't always get the answer you're looking for, but you will have Jesus, who is the answer. This is cliché and Sunday school, you might say. It certainly is if you don't understand the gravity of Jesus' presence in a situation. He may not reach out His hand and solve your problem with an answer to a lottery-ticket-type prayer. If He presents Himself, problems have a way of melting around us so He is in His proper place. When we place Jesus at the center of our focus, the problems that loomed so large over us sit directly under the feet of His absolute sovereignty.

My life's a mess, you might say. These problems *do* need to get solved; it can't go on like this forever. Perhaps the word you need is a word that will change you into the type of person who overcomes what is before you. It's possible that God will tell you from His word that it's time to grow up, to steward what's in front of you, that you are responsible for the mess itself, and at the very least you are responsible for how you feel and respond to the life you have before you.

You see, silence will pull all of these things out of you. I almost imagine it like I'm one of my kids. My youngest daughter especially does this and it's a delight; she'll walk up to me without a word and stick her hands up in the air. Every parent, in fact every human, knows exactly what that means. Dad, pick me up. Dad, you can carry me. I lay the weight of my sin, my mistakes, my frustrations, my challenges, defeats and victories, and I lift my hands in silence. My heart groans before God, and He knows exactly what I mean. "*Pick me up, Dad.*" I am entirely dependent on You. And until I got quiet and looked at the actual state of things, whether they are good or bad, I did not realize how much I actually needed You.

Silence lets the dross of our life, the fruitless, valueless garbage rise to the surface so by the sanctifying work of the Holy Spirit it can be skimmed from the surface to produce something of eternal value.

The truth is in many respects that we have no idea what we are actually wrestling with until we can get counsel from the Holy Spirit. We can so often be inundated with the noise of our self-talk that we can't hear through the static.

So what do you need? Lift up your hands, and even the things you cannot express with words will receive an answer. Your Father responds, "Let Me carry this for you, and let Me correct this for you." It is, after all, His delight to give you the Kingdom.

Third, in the midst of your retreat, whether it be an hour or a few days, eliminate distraction. Phones, mindless entertainment, anything that has a numbing effect. You need to be as sharp as possible. What I like to do is have a journal set aside specifically for distractions, especially when it comes to work. Write those things down quickly and get back to just being quiet and listening with your heart intent on God.

If you need worship music or instrumental music to get started, that's fine. People call this soaking; in the right context this can be helpful. I have found, though, that many of these "soaking" sessions are self-centered attempts at an experience and not a laying aside of time and space to hear directly from God in our hearts. That is what biblically practiced silence is for. We cannot manipulate and control the Holy Spirit like a tool; we must surrender to His will in this space, or we will miss the point entirely. To be with Him, to hear from Him, no matter what we experience.

How Do I Know It's God Talking?

Lastly, the question many ask here is, "How do I know that I'm hearing God?" There is a simple solution for this, and again, it comes with practice. If you can align what God is saying to you with scripture, you have a genuine word from the Lord. Now, many people will start looking for a chapter and verse to specifically align with what they are hearing. This does happen at times, but you need to understand the entire counsel of scripture so you can wrap your head and heart around what you are hearing in silence.

Take a specific situation, for example. You go on a retreat to get answers from God on your marriage, and you hear the thought formulated in your mind, "You were never meant to marry this person, they don't appreciate you enough, you need to be with someone else." Now can you find a chapter and verse that says you need to divorce Greg or separate from Alice? The Bible is brutally clear on divorce in multiple contexts. God hates it. So no, unless you are truly being abused or infidelity is evident, God did not tell you to get a divorce.

Or in the case of, "Should I marry this person?" Perhaps you do get a word from God on a particular person with whom you should pursue marriage. Great, as long as they reciprocate—otherwise, you are just creepy. In a majority of instances, this is just not the case. God loves marriage, and marriage is good; it is instituted at the beginning of creation by God Himself in the creation of Eve. So marriage itself is good. Scripture says you're in the clear. Now do people you trust agree, people who are truly following Christ? Does the spiritual authority in your life say yes? Is this person a believer themselves, or are you hoping to convert them?

When it comes to life's complications with relationships and work, getting a green light from God is important. Silence and stillness are not an excuse to ignore the entire counsel of scripture and the wisdom of those who can see into your life clearly. This is called stupidity and foolishness. If you can't sing and can't hear pitch, the word you got in your retreat that you'll lead thousands in worship is probably a dud.

The process of knowing you heard from the Lord? Scripture, wise people, and does it bear fruit that is in line with the Kingdom? Don't be too spooked by this aspect; you'll certainly make mistakes. Continue to practice, keep tuning in to the Lord's voice. Become a student of scripture and of those who have lived godly lives before you. Whatever you do, don't give up! Silence is a gift that will help you navigate through life following Jesus like few others. Combined with prayer, with the word, and with simple sacrifice, you'll begin to look forward to these times with the Lord. Silence in His presence will begin to shape your life in ways you can't now imagine.

Remember to get alone, and get quiet. You won't regret it.

The Path

Here is a quick, two-step process you can take in order to learn to be alone with God.

1. Set aside the daily time when your residence is most quiet, set aside the space, and get alone with God daily. Alone means no phone and no distractions.

2. Set a date in the calendar, two times a year, when you spend an extended amount of

time alone. Get away from technology—either from the temptation to work or to outright sin when you are alone.

Put everything in your calendar. Treat Jesus like a person you are meeting with, honor Him with your time, and you will receive the honor of His presence in return.

Chapter 10

SEX

*As citizens, they share in all things with others,
and yet endure all things as if foreigners. Every foreign land is to them as their native country, and
every land of their birth as a land of strangers.
They marry, as do all [others]; they beget children;
but they do not destroy their offspring. They have
a common table, but not a common bed. They are
in the flesh, but they do not live after the flesh.*
—The Epistle of Mathetes to Diognetus

What was once shameful has become common practice.
What was once for society's perverted and twisted is now
being praised when given to children. The abhorrent has

become sacred worship of the most debased and dishonorable kind. Dignity and honor for the image of God in people has been degraded to a point where it is now difficult to find. Whether the degradation is public or in the secret of our phones.

Our society worships sex, and children are sacrificed at the altar.

The church has in no way left this fight unscathed. Society constantly berates us with the belief that sex itself is the goal to a fulfilling life. Just pursue your desires—it's natural. Our churches are full of men and women who live a lifestyle so outside the biblical model that the seeker-sensitive movement has simply given in to the hedonistic onslaught of the world. The idiotic and unhelpful catchphrase "Love is love" is a typical example.

Pornography is a plague that has spread to unbelievable proportions, and websites like OnlyFans have gone even further to turn individual women into pay-for-play prostitutes and the men (and now becoming more common, women) who watch them into addicts. They slowly, and then quickly, are losing the ability to achieve real intimacy and fulfilment in sex.

I am particularly passionate about this. I was addicted to porn.

I grew up in a society without smartphones, as hard as that world is to imagine. To give you any idea how old I am as an "elder millennial," I remember when we first had the internet installed into our home. A world of information and communication was quickly capitalized on by those who realized the "oldest profession" would now require no level of public embarrassment, risk, or general creepiness. I saw my first *Playboy* magazine at a friend's house at the age of five. In that instance, I was shocked and told my parents. Needless to say that little friend was quickly not my little friend anymore. Right around the age of 13 (1999), the internet was just getting started. I began to dabble in the basic Victoria's Secret-type websites. In my late teens and into my early- to mid-20s, the smartphone changed all that. For many young men, that little screen has become a portal to hell, literal brain rot similar to that of an opioid addict, and a total saturation in unrealistic and, in most cases, abusive sex.

In my mid-twenties I also got free. It wasn't a complicated process. I got sick of myself and realized that this isn't what a man does. Then I fasted, prayed, repented, and invited Christ into every moment of temptation and failure. I then decided to get so busy chasing what I really wanted in life that I didn't have time or energy to dwell on temptation. Of course, the idea still raised its ugly head, but I replaced my sin with the habits you have been reading about in this book.

The Coward's Intimacy

In many ways my path in following Jesus and spiritual disciplines truly began in my freedom from, calling it what it is, sexual perversion and cowardice. That's right, cowardice as well. The fear of rejection plays an enormous role in pornography addiction. The desire for true intimacy with the opposite sex is a legitimate desire. The coward's way is to search for it on a phone, through a screen. Dealing with an actual person, a genuine human being, and having a relationship with them is difficult and requires courage. Commitment requires real passion, endurance, and discipline. Porn does not. Porn is the way of the coward.

The church is complicit in this in so many ways we cannot list them all. I will address the core issue—consumerism. Our God has become one of therapeutic deism. Not to be feared or revered as holy, but a love bug in the sky who makes our boo-boos go away and sweeps even our most egregious sins under the rug. He's a therapist who makes you feel good about yourself, and our pulpits send this message *ad nauseum* to fill a church or to fulfill the dream of being a social media "influencer." We have ignored God's holiness and His desires and boundaries around almost everything, why not sex?

I firmly believe we have lost strong male leadership and a generation of men in general due to our consumeristic attitude toward sex and life. Whenever you divorce freedom from responsibility, slavery is always the result. The world along with large swaths of the church have become obedient slaves to our appetites for more. We have been taken from our birthright to create, to be fruitful and multiply, and cheapened it to the point where consuming for the sake of consuming is actually held as an ideal to be pursued!

In the end, women and children suffer the most from a lack of strong men. The covenant of marriage protects the family. The traditional family unit is intended by God to protect the weaker sex and young children from the natural inclination of men toward violence and variety. Marriage channels that aggression and desire into overseeing and guiding the building blocks of a good and decent society. The intended purpose of sex is to bond a man to one wife, and her to him, and to produce children from pleasure and intimacy. To literally make the future from a God-ordained miracle. We have taken something that is a representation of the eternal nature of God (procreation) and turned it into an outlet for our brokenness and lack. This is not the way. We can see that it is not the way. So how do you, as an individual, practice following Jesus when it comes to sex?

First of all, it is not just a matter of waking up one day and deciding internally to no longer lust or fantasize (yes ladies, imagining you'll be with another woman's husband even in an innocent setting is fantasy). Many have decided that over and over and over again. The simple fact is you need a new brain. Luckily, God made your mind in a way that it can be transformed. Saying, "I am going to stop lusting" is not a helpful piece of advice or a good plan of attack. Keep in mind that's exactly what this is—a plan of attack. Sexual perversion must be unmasked and treated like the enemy it is. You must go to war.

Step 1: Unmask the Enemy

You cannot fight what you cannot see clearly. Sun Tzu says this in *The Art of War*: "If you know the enemy and know yourself, you need not fear the result of a hundred battles. If you know yourself but not the enemy, for every victory gained you will also suffer a defeat. If you know neither the enemy nor yourself, you will succumb in every battle."

Know your enemy and know that your enemy hates you and hates sex. I do not mean a level of hatred that you can comprehend in this life. Your enemy wants you to suffer horribly and to die for all of eternity. That is day after day of absolute darkness and suffering kind of hatred. The little treats he is giving you all have hooks that sink into your heart and draw you toward hell. He hates you and the God you serve, and your enemy should be treated as such. The devil gives no quarter, you must be ruthless and give none in return.

> *Therefore, confess your sins to one another and pray for one another, that you may be healed. The prayer of a righteous person has great power as it is working* (James 5:16 ESV).

Simply tell someone. Not to make yourself feel better and not as an accountability partner whom you end up having to confess to innumerable times. Nor to a group of men or women who simply talk about their most recent failure with no plan of action to combat it. You need to confess—with a broken heart you need to confess.

Step 2: Forgive

At some point your enemy the devil got his hooks in you with offense. This may seem unrelated to sexual perversion, until you note that close to 80 percent of all pornography online involves punishing or violating a woman in some way. There is a disdain that many have held on to for the opposite sex. Search your heart and find out right where that started, and forgive that person. Not "people" or that gender in general; forgive the actual person who did not live up to your expectations, hurt you, abused you, or was violent toward you. I understand—this part is hard. You cannot allow the sins or shortcomings of another person in your past to ruin your life right now. To be victimized is a horrible thing; to be a victim for the rest of your life is an insult to the work Christ has done and is doing in you. Forgive. Burn out the bitterness. Nobody owes you anything in this life. Remember, you're a creator, not a consumer; a giver, not a thief.

Step 3: Don't Just Remove, Replace

Habits are stubborn things. We are wired to have them, and so much of our daily lives is automatic behavior. Habits are a double-edged sword. Jesus illustrates this point well.

> *When the unclean spirit has gone out of a person, it passes through waterless places seeking rest, but finds none. Then it says, "I will return to my house from which I came." And when it comes, it finds the house empty, swept, and put in order. Then it goes and brings with it seven other spirits more evil than itself, and they enter and dwell there, and the last state of that person is worse than the first. So also will it be with this evil generation* (Matthew 12:43-45 ESV).

In this case, Jesus is using exorcism as a metaphor for an entire generation. I believe we see this play out in our personal lives when it comes to sexual temptation. We think we have a handle on it, then all of a sudden the flood gates open again and we give in to the onslaught.

We have to be diligent in filling our house with good things. What are the triggers that drive your addiction or fantasy when it comes to sex? Take note, that's the door. It does not have to be something like a movie or TV show that shows some skin. It can be as simple as loneliness, or melancholy the day after a big personal win, or an argument with a friend or spouse, or a terrible day. Whatever it is, take note of it and begin to replace your habit.

Lonely? Call a friend or loved one. Don't have any friends? Go to a gym and ask some advice from someone—have a conversation with a real person. Had a huge win in ministry or work the day before? You'll come down off of that high eventually. Plan to go see something beautiful. It may be art or nature, but refill your soul and get refreshed instead of wallowing. Just finished an argument with your spouse over the phone? Do something petty like hide the remote or leave the dishes to "soak" instead of just cleaning them (kidding). Take some time to cool down away from your devices—walk, pray, drive, and while you're at it do something kind for them.

These are obviously just examples. Pick your positive poison when it comes to replacing habits. This is an absolute key to walking in purity and to life in general. We are habitual creatures and emotional creatures; we are rarely logical.

You cannot simply stop a habit; it has to be replaced. Quitting something means starting something else.

Fourth and finally (don't worry, there are less than 12 steps):

Step 4: Completely Submit Every Aspect of Your Life to Christ

This seems obvious, but have you laid every aspect of your life before Him and said simply, "Do thy will"?

This is an active, not a passive step toward freedom. As a church we have been so wrapped up in the accumulation of knowledge that we know all the things to do and are so busy learning more we have no willpower left to do them.

Surrender plays an active and daily role in your life. This is what is at the core of what we call faith. In the sense the New Testament uses this word, it can be far more related to fealty to a king than believing something great is about to happen. Biblical faith is faith in God, not in our own ability to have faith in something. We know that despite our failures, the Jesus we see in the Bible keeps His promises and does the real heavy lifting. We submit to that work and to the Holy Spirit with our words, actions, and habits.

If we read the word, do we do what it says? If we pray and hear from the Lord, do we lean on Him to accomplish it? If we sin, do we trust Him to forgive us and remove our (correctly felt) shame? Where does your trust lie for your freedom? Don't be a foolish Galatian—don't be bewitched into thinking willpower will save you. It did not do so at first and it will not now. Surrender of your will to God is truly your only hope.

You are a living, breathing work of art. A creation. The painting does not make itself—it falls under the master's brush.

You were saved by grace and faith, both given to you alone. In this instance it is the same. To be set free you must lift up your hands, as chained as they may be, and cry out for mercy from God. He always is available to those who truly seek Him.

You can and will be free from sexual sin. You will also find that in being set free from perversion, sex within the bounds of marriage actually fills you up with connection and intimacy. As strange as it sounds, it will be an act of submission and worship to God Himself. God is not blushing at your desires, and He desires for you to live an absolutely full life, which includes good sex. You will no longer be a consumer but a giver, no longer be a thief but a creator. Any sex outside of marriage is based on a lie that it will fill you up—that it's the goal, the end all be all. No, sex is a passionate, human, and raging fire that God uses to warm an entire household with genuine life. Like a fire, it can either provide warmth, comfort, and pleasure, or it can burn your house down.

God set boundaries around it to make it good, to make it otherworldly in your experience. Not to limit you.

Now a short piece of practice. Go and discuss this chapter with your husband or wife, if you are married, and present your expectations when it comes to sex. Then pray together about your sex life.

If you are unmarried, pray for your future spouse, whoever they are. This may seem like a silly thing to modern ears. What the world deems foolish is a good indicator of exactly what you should be doing to live a fulfilling life in Christ.

Take the narrow path.

The Path

Confess and Repent

The first step to genuine sexual freedom is many times the hardest to come to grips with.

First, confess to the person who would be most betrayed by sexual misconduct (if you have any). Second, repent to the spiritual leadership in your life and ask for their help in setting the course right. Do not allow "little things" or "little slips" to fool you. It's all sin. Confess, repent, and get going.

Forgive, and Give No Quarter

Offense, surprisingly, is many times the issue the enemy uses to gain access to our life when it comes to sexual sin. Or, in the very least, a sense of entitlement. Nobody owes you sexual gratification. If this is an issue with your spouse, be honest about it and bring it to a neutral party if need be.

Make a list of the people you need to forgive who have wounded you in the past. Give the decision of their judgment over to God.

Be ruthless in your assessment. Give no quarter to the enemy.

Replace

Find out what triggers your addiction, if you have one. Also, find out what triggers the "little slips" you have when it comes to sex and even fantasy about relationships. What are you doing? Where are you? How are you feeling? How has your time in the word and prayer been?

Now choose the habit that will replace this.

It could be opening a book, prayer, exercise, a call or text to a loved one, or going for a walk. This may seem stupidly simple, but that is how the human brain works.

Chapter 11

MONEY

So if you have not been trustworthy in handling
worldly wealth, who will trust you with true riches?
—Luke 16:11 NIV

If someone walked into the room you're sitting in right now and handed you a check for your personal use for 1 million dollars, would you know what to do with it?

Let's call it the million-dollar question. Maybe that's a lot of money to you, or maybe you live in a major city where it would buy you a one bedroom apartment that's really just a converted studio. Either way, I think this question reveals a lot about our desires.

You have a relationship with money. It may be dysfunctional, ambivalent, or healthy and biblical. The fact remains, we all need it, and we all need to make our peace with that fact. You may not think of anything to do with money as a spiritual discipline, but here's where you'd be wrong. Jesus talks about money more than faith and prayer combined in the gospels. This gives me the sneaking suspicion that God really cares about what we do with it and how we steward it.

My personal relationship with money has been dysfunctional up until just a few years ago, and we're still working out the kinks. We still argue now and again, but for the most part we have made our peace. I endeavor to one day say what Paul the apostle states in Philippians 4:11-13 (ESV):

> *Not that I am speaking of being in need, for I have learned in whatever situation I am to be content. I know how to be brought low, and I know how to abound. In any and every circumstance, I have learned the secret of facing plenty and hunger, abundance and need. I can do all things through him who strengthens me.*

For the most part, that "I can do all things through Christ who strengthens me" is used as a catch-all for being able to do impossible things for Jesus. What Paul is actually aiming at here is letting the Philippian church know that he's thankful for the financial gift that they sent, but if they don't provide, God will and the job will get done because Jesus is the one who is really in control, and Paul is content with that.

There are two ends of the spectrum when it comes to money that I will use as extremes to make a point. Try your best to avoid placing yourself outside these categories of idolatry even though I am using hyperbole to force my argument. We all live in this space somewhere and need to land where God wants us to when it comes to money—living as good stewards of a temporal tool that is used to expand the eternal Kingdom.

Here are the categories we all fall into at some point more or less, and both can leave us stranded on the rocks, shipwrecked and grasping for something that simply floats.

1. The unsatisfied and rich worshiper of mammon
2. The unsatisfied and poor worshiper of mammon

When I speak here about dissatisfaction, I'm not talking about a holy and righteous fervor that drives us closer to the King and out of our placid and boring routine Christianity. That is a good dissatisfaction and it should be steeped in like a good pot of cowboy coffee in the wild. Let it be as thick and as potent as possible, and drink it to the dregs.

The dissatisfaction I'm speaking about is the kind that is thankful for very little, frustrated at their current financial position in life, envious of others' success and happiness, and constantly accumulating "stuff" to fill some kind of gaping hole in their heart.

Both types are frustrated, and both types serve the same god of money whether they are aware of it or not.

Take a moment and truly look at your life when it comes to money and your relationship with it. Is there any part of you that is envious of others' gain? Any portion of you that hates the rich simply for the fact that they have more than you? Is there part of you that can't let go of your possessions, whether it be wealth or even control of relationships? Is there any part of you that *needs* to accumulate the things of this earth without a thought toward eternal reward?

Simply put, whether it is a lot or a little, is money keeping you from full communion with Jesus? This is not a judgment on the rich or the poor. It is a judgment of the heart. Where are your true riches? You may never be rich and, God bless you, you may never be broke, but where is your heart?

There is a simple answer to break free from this cycle and from this false god. If you serve God with your life and habits, everything in you will tell you that this is not the way. That what I am about to say is Old Testament or religious or pharisaical. That, in short, you are entitled to your feelings and your patterns of behavior. But if you really want to be free, this is where you will start. Tithe.

There is a lot of talk in this generation about whether or not this is a New Testament concept. It is clearly a biblical principle that fits the entire narrative of scripture, and those who deny it are usually stingy and not trying with all their might to find a way to be New Testament generous (sell everything and lay it at the apostles' feet). But here, let's just view it simply as a spiritual discipline.

When you learn to give your money, specifically, to your local church, you take yourself out of the position of victim and beggar and into the position of provider and giver. You are acknowledging the fact that it is God who provides and cares for your needs.

The Unsatisfied Rich Worshiper of Mammon

The reality is that this person lives inside all of us. This person has everything they need and more, yet for some reason they cannot seem to be satisfied with what they have, *even great gains in financial accumulation.* They lay their lives at the altar of mammon. By that I mean their true lives, the things that give them life. The altar of mammon has strewn before it the carnage of families, marriages, children, churches, ministries, careers, and as a result sometimes entire lives. This man or woman must accumulate, and this means financial gain and people for their own purposes.

Aren't you tired of being sold a life that will never fill you? Aren't you exhausted from the hustle and the striving for some paradise that doesn't exist? Haven't we learned that accumulation and wealth aren't the measure of a life well lived?

Wealth is a neutral quality that lies in the hands of the character of the person who possesses it. Money is neutral. Wealth is not wrong like a gun is not "wrong." A gun does whatever the person holding it decides to use it for. Will it defend my home and my country? Or will it destroy homes and my country? Wealth is the same, and there is nothing wrong with having wealth, even immense wealth. Abraham, Isaac, Jacob, David, Solomon, and Job were famously wealthy, filthy rich, yet it was their faith and their heart that God judged, not their possessions.

The difference lies in who you worship with your wealth and whether or not you begin to worship the wealth itself.

Holy dissatisfaction is one thing; desiring wealth simply to add value and status to yourself is idol worship.

Let's put this in perspective. God made everything with a word. He probably finds it first hilarious and then concerning that human beings spend so much of their time, energy, and effort accumulating something that they can't even take with them when they die. Think of it—when God made the universe He spoke gold and diamonds and all things precious and valuable into existence with a word. We may spend our lives accumulating the things He simply spoke and created, laying our lives and our families and relationships on the altar in order to do so.

And that's how you can tell you are worshiping mammon. What are you willing to lay on the altar for it? We live in a world that pushes hustle on every media platform. Get after it, be better, wake up earlier, travel more, get wealthy at all costs, and be the best *you* you can be. This is stupid when removed from the context of Kingdom generosity. If you can't give it away, that possession owns you, you don't own it.

On the other hand, money can be a great tool to advance the Kingdom of Heaven on earth. Go ahead, be rich, be embarrassingly rich. *But give like there is no tomorrow.* Because as a matter of fact, there may not be.

As believers in an Almighty God who rules the universe and gave us the Bible, perhaps we can find a solution to the "financial worship crisis" that the world finds itself in. The solution is certainly not to aim to be broke so that people feel sorry for us or to be wealthy simply for status and accumulation. The path that Jesus lays out is radical, but in the light of cyclical historical rises and falls of empires, it makes complete sense.

> *Do not lay up for yourselves treasures on earth, where moth and rust destroy and where thieves break in and steal, but lay up for yourselves treasures in heaven, where neither moth nor rust destroys and where thieves do not break in and steal* (Matthew 6:19-20 ESV).

Give in an honorable way. Store up an inheritance for your children's children (that's generational wealth, by the way). Be honest in all your dealings. Care for orphans and widows. Steward what you have been given with the fear of the Lord in your heart. Be skillful and contribute as a citizen of your nation. Enjoy quality over quantity. Give everything its proper place in relation to money. If it occupies your mind and gives you anxiety, you are fearing the increase or fearing the decrease and not fearing the *God who made it.*

It's God who gives us the ability to make wealth. Money is a terrible master but a useful servant. Do not let it rule you.

That means the basics. Budgeting, investment, and assets for generational wealth. Everyone's ability to do this will be different, depending on so many variables it will make your head spin. Not all minds or all skills are created equal, no matter what economy you are in. But you can find a way to honor God with your work and with your money. That truly is what generosity is all about. The time you have spent earning an income is laid at the altar in order to honor God with your work and your increase. This is the first step. This puts you in a position not as a beggar or a victim, but as someone who has the ability to give. The mindset change when it comes to generosity is miraculous.

The Unsatisfied Poor Worshiper of Mammon

The issue this comes down to is covetousness. It is blazoned on social media with catchphrases like, "Eat the rich." Wanting what someone else has does not give you the "right" to hold contempt and bitterness in your heart. Someone who goes without can be just as much a worshiper of money as someone who lives in plenty.

I remember when my wife, Jessi, and I first moved to California and we simply could not pay rent on time for several months. We were broke. We decided, as a family, that we would give to God first anyway. It was not the money we were after, but the mentality that we will never bend the knee to financial circumstances or the bait of consumerism. We would give, no matter what, and put ourselves in a position to do so.

This is the way out of worshiping money when you are broke. Start to give however you can. This pulls you into gratitude and being a contributor and out of a mindset of lack and envy.

"But Parker, what about the people who have nothing? Why would you tell them that? They need to take care of their families." This line of reasoning is offensive to God our Father.

Do you honestly believe that He won't keep His word? That He won't take care of His children in this life and the life to come? Do you have so little faith that you think generosity only works for those with the readily available means to do so and not for those with very little means to do so?

I had a conversation about curses in developing nations with a friend of mine, Ben Hughes. We offer the free gift of salvation (excellent!), but we almost never ask for the believers present to give to the work that is being done. Why? We don't have faith that God will provide for the poor when they are generous. It only works in a less corrupt and less broken system. We turn these people into victims and needy orphans by not revealing the truth that God takes care of His own no matter the circumstances. Will they still be poor? Maybe. Will they still struggle? Almost certainly. But what about their kids? What if they see their mother or father who has to walk a mile to get fresh water giving the first part of their income to the work of the Kingdom? That's how generational wealth begins. You teach a generation that when you give to God, you invest in eternity. When you invest in what is even more tangible than the world we live in, you teach with your actions that Christ is seated in heavenly places and that you are seated with Him. After all, what does a child of God have to worry about? We aren't to be concerned with death itself, what are we doing worrying about money? That is dumb.

Here is some helpful advice. Live below your means, no matter how great your means are. If you are barely scraping by, the best thing to do in any economy is to improve or gain new skills. Useful skills never lose value no matter the context. When it comes to your budget, put God first, your family second, and everything else a distant third. Priority reveals your values. Where your money goes, there your heart is, after all, and not vice versa.

Learn to invest. This does not mean gambling; it means investing. Learn something about how money works, and educate yourself on how to handle it. Then invest in something you actually understand. If you are pitched a deal to invest your hard-earned money into something that you don't understand, get away. Either learn about it first or just say no. A simple rule is to look for something that makes your money work and produces more money without you having to spend time doing it. Almost everyone in the world has access to information and principles on how to create some level of wealth. But you don't have a money problem, you have a worship problem. You get emotional about money because you think you need it. Put yourself in a position where your services and your investments bring money to you. This is being a master over your money as a steward instead of being mastered by it.

Lastly, generational wealth. This is mostly transferred in principles, not in the finances themselves. Families that are afraid of money find very often that money is afraid of them. Teach the generations what to do with it when it comes and teach them early. Keep it simple. Money is not to be feared, only God is. Are you afraid of money? Well then, there is probably a part of you that worships it still. Generational wealth is built first spiritually, and it does not matter how much you have to start that process. I know that in my family, growing up, we were mostly finding ourselves struggling financially. You know what I got anyway? A spiritual inheritance, toughness, and a mentality of overcoming. Being poor doesn't mean you don't have anything. In fact, many people who are poor have far more than those who are rich (but not all—many impoverished people are still full of sin and truly have nothing and no hope; that's why the gospel is the first need that needs to be met). Learn to treat money like a tool to advance the Kingdom and care for your family. It is not a thing that should affect us deeply emotionally.

The issue with money is a simple one, but for many a difficult wrestle. Not everyone will be rich, but everyone can be rich toward God. Wealth in the Kingdom is not necessarily seen as "How much do you have?" but more "What did you do with what you were given?"

In conclusion, neither poverty nor great accumulation of wealth are inherently holy. What matters is how you honor God with your wealth in the end. Truly, in the end. You will not be judged based on what someone else had or be compared to another. You will be judged based on what you did with what you were given. This is the focal point of stewardship in the Bible. Everything that you have has been given to you. Gifts, talents, ability, upbringing, all of it. So now, what will you do with that in order to stay on the path?

The choice is yours.

The Path

As almost everyone knows, money needs a plan before it arrives in your bank account so that you are managing your money and it's not managing you.

Whether you have a lot or a little, here is what I suggest. Sit down with your spouse, if you have one, and write these down.

1. Pray and Begin Tithing

Money can be a sticky issue for many people. It's best to invite God and His word into your financial planning. What He says goes. Everyone has different gifts, values, and goals; these first need to align with what God wants you to do with your money.

You should immediately begin giving to your local church; this is the first step in biblical generosity. If you don't want to tithe, that's fine; go with the New Testament standard—sell everything, and lay it at the feet of your spiritual leaders with no strings attached.

2. *Write Down Your Values*

What are your *actual* values when it comes to money? Investment for the future? Memorable experiences? Over the top generosity? Frugality? Luxury?

Write a few down and then find common ground if you're "negotiating" with a spouse.

3. *Set Financial Goals*

This may seem obvious, but most people don't have them. The way my wife and I do this is that we choose an amount at the beginning of each year that we would like to give away. The fact that you are tithing to your local church should go without saying. How much over and above that do you want to give? Generosity is the main thrust of our financial goal setting. We find our needs are well taken care of since this mindset shift.

4. *Write Down a Budget*

This is another obvious one, but very rarely seen practice. Use whatever system you need to. If your income fluctuates, use a percentage system in order of biblical values. Our basic order is: give, invest, take care of needs, vacation saving, holiday saving, wants or extra toward goals. This is simple, and life throws curve balls, but at least you can be ready for them when they come.

5. *Be Grateful*

Cultivate a sense of gratitude for every single solitary thing that happens to you. This is often learned in difficulty, but it doesn't have to be. Start a list of things you are grateful for. You can start with intangibles, but when it comes to actual provision from God, celebrate it like crazy. You may seem crazy to your friends, but if you're going to be rich, be joyful, and if you end up broke, be joyful.

Chapter 12

HONOR YOUR FATHER AND MOTHER

Children, obey your parents in the Lord, for this is right. "Honor your father and mother" (this is the first commandment with a promise), "that it may go well with you and that you may live long in the land."
—EPHESIANS 6:1-3 ESV

This will be a difficult chapter, and I am warning you of this in advance. I have found this principle alone will cause the most emotion I have seen for those who want to follow the path that Jesus lays out for us. You will be "triggered" by the advice Jesus and His apostles give us when it comes to honoring our fathers and mothers—both physical, adopted, and spiritual. Why? Because we have invested by far the most expectations in these authority figures in our life, so they also have the opportunity to fail us in the most disastrous ways.

You will find that taking personal responsibility for honor will be one of the hardest things that you have to do in your life. This is why I am writing about it in a book about the practical, daily path in following Jesus and truly finding Him, and why it's the second to last chapter. I wanted you to keep reading and not throw the book across the room and tell your friends and your spouse how ridiculous I am.

One of the main principles, if not the very core principle of honor, is the fact that it is not based on the behavior of those you are commanded to honor but your personal behavior and Christ-like response to their actions. God will not judge you or cut you slack based on how someone else behaved but on how you *respond* to the behavior of others. This is a horrible reality for most. The self-righteousness in all of us rails against this. We see ourselves above and beyond our parents and (especially failed) spiritually leaders. We are separate, apart from them, doing something better and different.

The fact is, this is never the case when we harbor bitterness and judgment against those God has placed in our life to lead us and raise us. We can live with our eyes wide open with regard to human frailty, brokenness, and even cruelty while continuing to be joyful, forgiving, shrewd, and wise when it comes to how we live our lives. How your life turns out and how you follow Jesus is not up to anyone else. Not one person will stand before the great white throne on the day of judgment for your actions but you. Allowing God to judge our teachers (good or bad) is a difficult thing to do, but we must if we wish to follow the true path of Christ.

By honoring your father and mother, you are, in fact, honoring yourself.

Do you remember the first time you realized your parents were, in fact, just people? With their own sets of strengths and weaknesses, their own victories and failures. Parents are far from perfect, just like you are far from perfect. The reality is every child of every parent has unmet expectations, and there are needs in every heart that can only be met by God. That is why it's my opinion that the best parenting puts children on a path to find God in the word and in experiencing Him in family life and within the church. There are simply no perfect parents; many are far from that.

What honoring your father and mother is *not* is trying to change your parents—spiritual, biological, or adoptive. It is a matter of honoring the fact that you came from them, that they gave you life, and that God chose them to raise you whether they did an excellent job of it or a complete mess or anything in between. God gives us parents and we don't choose them. How we respond to them and treat them will determine the course of our lives in ways we cannot even imagine. In this chapter, we won't just be discussing the parents who raised you in your home but the importance of honoring spiritual parents as well, despite their flaws.

My parents loved me very well. They raised us in an environment in which we truly were treasured and looked after when it comes to all the things a young child could look for in a parent. They encouraged interest in God and in church, and they kept their marriage together despite having every reason to lay it down and go their separate ways. You see, when I was a child what I didn't know was that infidelity was a central theme of my parents' life leading up to the time I was born. It wasn't just some affair, but it involved the man who ran the small house church we attended for all of my young childhood. This group, looking back, really functioned more like a cult than a church.

In reality, I had no idea that any of this had taken place until I was in my early twenties, at Bible college in Australia, and living with my sister and brother-in-law there. My sister sat me down and gave me the nuts and bolts of the story. I wish I had responded with tears, or frustration, or pure hatred and anger, which would have been reasonable responses at that point. Instead, at that moment, it just made things make sense when I looked back on all the things in my life that seemed to plague me. My mother and my father, up until that point, had been loving parents who were focused on their family, doing their best financially to provide for us, and raising four kids (who all turned out to be great). Now, they were people, not just my parents. Probably the strongest feeling that I had at that moment was, "Then I will have to make a new way. I'll have to do it alone."

The reason I mention this part of the story is that in that moment my parents became absolutely human. The flaws and the cracks of humanity, their own shattered hopes and dreams, their anger or manipulation—all of this made sense. It also dawned on me that by the grace of God they had done the impossible. They had kept a marriage together, raised four kids, and laid down their expectations for life for the brutal reality they had both created and been the victims of. There was a choice to be made at this moment. Would I make the excuse that my parents were flawed and therefore I had a right to separate myself from them and point fingers at them for my own failures? Or would I honor them despite the mess? Are flaws and sin an excuse to set aside the commandment to honor them, or would I do what scripture asked for?

Remove the Complication

In many ways, this is one of the most complicated things to get right on the path. After all, Jesus says, "If you love Me, you'll keep My commandments." Many people will make the excuse that they have been hurt, that they have been victims, or that complete moral failure gives them the "right" to set aside this commandment and give room for offense and hatred. We have to remember that in the moments we choose to honor, our actions are far more about us than they are about the person we are honoring.

We do not have to live like them or set aside abuse and vile moral behavior—that is not the point. What we can do is choose to be honorable *despite* the reality of our parental and spiritual upbringing because that's what Jesus asks us to do.

How then does this really play out? First of all, you have to realize that the commandment to honor your father and mother is far more about you than it is about the condition of your parents or your spiritual leader. Whether you like it or not, honoring your parents is in fact a way of honoring yourself. They are a part of you. So when you honor them you bless yourself.

Every single man at some point makes the intention clear that they are separate from their parents (see Matthew 19:5)—the whole, "I am not my father" attitude. In one sense, this is absolutely true and absolutely healthy. A man shall cleave to his wife, and they shall become one. You truly become a separate household. But also in another sense, you are connected whether you like it or not.

I remember, growing up, a particular phrase my father would say that would drive me absolutely insane, "Because I said so." I was always a "why" kid. *Why* this and *why* that. Now I know exactly how my dad felt. At the end of a day of work, when you've been slogging away, explaining every reason behind a simple request to get something done around the house is not something you want to do. If I tell my boys to clean up their toys and they ask why, well, will they understand the reason if I tell them? "Well son, the reality is that you need to clean things up, leave things better than you found them, and put your own house in order because it teaches you valuable life lessons about almost every facet of your existence that will positively affect your future." A five-year-old doesn't care about their future in that way; they just want what they want when they want it. So "because I said so" has inadvertently slipped out of my mouth now on far too many occasions to count.

I am not saying that this is the right way to parent, but what I have realized is that I have far more of my mother and my father *in me* than I would like to admit or imagine. For another example, I forget things all the time. I get so focused on the next task at hand (or so I like to tell myself) that I will consistently leave things behind. This is something my mom does as well, and for some reason, in my infinite intelligence and wisdom, it drives me nuts when she does. You know why? Because, guess what, I hate when I do it myself. It reminds me of my fallible nature. It's embarrassing to have to drive back to places and waste people's time because I forgot something. It makes me feel stupid. I promise I am not a stupid person, but I certainly forget things.

I've also inherited other things from my parents—things that don't drive me crazy. Like my father's work ethic, my mother's ability to have fun, both of their pastoral and loving hearts for broken and hurting people. A love for music from my mom (she played the piano when I was growing up), a love for work and blue-collar humor from my dad. You get it all, and you don't always get to choose. You are shaped by them whether you like it or not. Sure, you can make your own path, and chart your own course, and by God you should! But to honor your father and mother *is to honor yourself* in what they have given you.

What About My Pastor?

The same goes for the spiritual authority that has been placed in your life. It goes without saying that just like your parents, at some point they will fail you. Spiritual parents are a precious gift, and whether for better or for worse they shaped you. We have to take into account the story of David when he was literally being hunted by his both governmental and spiritual leader. What did David do? He honored the fact that God had anointed this man to lead Israel. He honored the position of "father of Israel" even if the man himself had completely lost it and was out to murder him. This may seem extreme and make no sense at all to the modern westerner, but there is genius in it.

David knew that one day he would be king. Samuel had anointed him to be king. Word had started to get around as David approached his thirties and continued to excel that this would one day be the case. What if David had completely dishonored Saul? What if he had taken the course of libel and slander to unseat him and undermine his authority? Well, David would, in the end, be doing the same thing to himself. He would be placing the mistrust of the people of Israel not just in Saul (who was indeed failing as king) but in the *office* of the king itself. So what would happen when David took power? He would have people who were ready to make him king simply because he was different from the former king. This constantly happens in ministry. You may have every right to speak poorly of your former or current spiritual leader, but that does not make it right. We constantly lay our hands on the Lord's anointed with a grievous inability to see our own flaws and misconceptions. This is why David clearly states, "How dare I lay a hand on the Lord's anointed?"

In our case, it would very rarely come to actual physical violence like in David's position. Although we have no problem placing violence upon those whom God has anointed to lead for their very human flaws. Human beings tend to much more easily find flaws in others than in themselves. Especially when it comes to those who lead us. It's easy from a distance to find the flaws in our leaders and pronounce judgment. This is when we do the most violence to the body of Christ. Our words and actions tear down those we refuse to confront biblically, and unlike David we don't have the courage to either openly have conflict or repent of our actions. When they sin, we judge; yet all judgment in this regard should be placed in the hands of God, those placed in authority to guide the church in the case of moral failing, and the government God has put in place in the case of lawbreaking spiritual leaders. In a very real sense, the best thing that we can do is take what good we learned from those who have led us in the past, and discard that which is unscriptural and abusive. The best leaders you will ever have in your life are those who will teach you what *not* to do. Sauls are spiritual leaders, properly anointed, who lose their way. When they lead us, they teach us that anointing is not the end all be all of ministry, that character is the highest value, and that maintaining a humble spirit before God is real Christian progress.

Sauls can be our earthly fathers and mothers as well. They have been given to us by providence. They may be amazing, and they may be catastrophic failures and everything in between. They teach us what to do and what not to do. At the very least, they gave you life, a chance to make a difference on this earth by the very fact that you are living and breathing. The fact that they stewarded you (a gift to them, from God) well or poorly will be excruciatingly judged by God. He takes the raising of children seriously, so take comfort in that. You can learn from them, you can glean from them, and in an act that is supremely Christlike you can honor them. This can only come from a place of deep revelation that God is your true Father and He is perfect in every way. This places your mind and your heart above the fray of victimhood and into the space of a good servant of your Father in heaven who is loved and has access to eternal resources.

I have been led, directly or indirectly, by men who have been abusive to their congregations, slept with their parishioners and interns, openly manipulated people, underpaid their staff, and generally been poor shepherds. These same men taught me the word, encouraged me, and showed me kindness and compassion in regard to my walk in Christ as a young man. Should I throw it out because they fell? Should I not take the word that they bestowed upon me under the anointing God gave them? Should I dishonor them publicly and take justice into my own hands? Of course not. In these cases, I was not in a position to bring church discipline, nor could I have handled that burden (or want it, now that I have been in a position to do so).

Honor the position in the Kingdom and the anointing. In doing so you honor and bless yourself. This does not mean you should continue to be abused or tolerate affairs and indiscretion; it doesn't mean stay quiet when sin is obviously present. It means that in our cellular families and our spiritual families, honor holds reward for you despite the imperfection of those who raise us and lead us.

You may be wondering now why this is in a book about spiritual disciplines. Well, you may have guessed this already. To honor a human being in a position of spiritual authority (most notably spiritual and physical fathers) takes real work in the presence of God and His word. As the old adage goes, "Never meet your heroes." You will realize that they are flawed and imperfect just like you. You can choose to take this as an encouragement or a great disappointment. I choose to take it as encouragement. If God can use them, He can use me. It does not mean you're the same or that you have been given the same authority or failings. But it does mean that God uses human beings to accomplish His will despite their weaknesses, and in many cases He uses their weaknesses to glorify Himself.

You will be grateful you did this when your time for promotion does come. Until you hold the weight of responsibility and encounter the level of temptation these people have had in life, you simply cannot understand their outcomes.

Again, this does not mean immoral behavior is to be honored or hidden under a rug. Paul the apostle tells Timothy to announce publicly the immoral behavior and the disciplinary actions taken to the whole church so that "they may live in fear." That's right—so that people will be afraid to sin in the church. Remember, though, Paul was speaking from a place of apostolic authority. It's good to honestly assess what your role would be in exposing sin and to do it in an honorable way. In fact, honoring that position and anointing of a person may mean bringing things to light in some cases.

So how do we actually honor our fathers and mothers?

First: With Our Words

If you can do this, you can do anything. This includes how we speak about people on any media platform. Unfortunately for justice and truth oriented people like me, this means that we pray for them when they become our enemies. Especially when they become our enemies.

There are good and bad parents, good and bad pastors. There is one person you are responsible for when it comes to how you respond to them—you.

Use your words in every situation possible to encourage your parents. Use your words to encourage your pastor. In most cases you have no idea what they are facing on a daily basis. Speak well of them to others and don't allow hearsay and gossip to be spoken in your presence. For the most part people will tell you that about me. If gossip about pastors, parents, or friends takes place around me, the silence or my response will ruin a whole evening with awkwardness. I don't allow it, especially if facts aren't confirmed.

I know it's hard to imagine in a world where our lives are made public, but many of us simply need to learn to mind our own business. Most pastors and parents are doing their best and doing quite well. After all, you never hear about the tens of thousands of flights that land safely on a daily basis; you hear about the disasters.

Use your words for good. For encouragement. And when facts are confirmed, refer to Matthew 18 for a process that is built for restoration if the sinful party is willing to participate. Blasting someone on social media or to your friends or even your spouse is not biblical. I have never seen this produce good fruit in the life of a believer. Never.

Be honorable with your words, be truthful in everything you say, and honor the anointing a person has been given. After all, you may be given that same position of authority in the future; how would you want someone to treat you in that case?

Second: With Our Actions

The Western world has a problem with the elderly. We have a problem with our history and with our parents. We tuck them away—or throw them away, in many cases—into institutions far from family and from human dignity. We do the same with pastors who are no longer "relevant." The speaking invitations dry up, they are considered irrelevant or senile, and we push aside their contributions and their stories for the "new thing."

Jesus angrily rebukes this attitude in the Pharisees. They would make a practice of giving to the temple or the "work of God" while neglecting to honor the more important thing. The commandment—yes, the *command*—to honor your father and mother. Your most important action contains your two most valuable assets in life—your time and your money. Simply put, your money can also be seen as a gift of time. For most people, time truly is money. The time you work is paid through wages that represent time.

Are you spending time with them, and are you investing on their behalf? When your parents or your pastor can no longer do what is considered productive work, have you made plans to advocate for their honor and human dignity? Again, how would you wish to be honored in this case?

The caveat, of course, is if any of these people are a danger to you or your immediate family. I am not recommending giving time and money to people who are decidedly evil. In most cases, which is a relief, this is simply not the case. We just tend to purposefully "forget" and move on.

This is one of the glaring problems in my generation and those that follow. They have no sense of history and no sense of place. So they are making it up as they go along. This does not need to be the case. Whether learning from a faithful life well-lived or a total train wreck, a sense of the history contained in individuals who have lived their lives needs to be brought to the forefront. Too many people talk about "multi-generational" churches. What they mean is they want young people to come. But who will lead them? Who will teach them the hard lessons? Who will remind them that life is short? Honor those who have gone before us, despite their flaws.

When it comes to your parents and your spiritual parents, how are you honoring them with your actions? What are you teaching your children and those around you about how they should treat *you* when you are no longer healthy, capable, or "relevant"? How we treat the elderly and aging ministers and parents in our society is a crime that needs to be corrected. And it starts with you.

The Path

Here are some very practical ways to do this. The caveat here is if your father and mother are literally physically unsafe for you or your family to be around. Use wisdom.

1. Forgive

This is step number one to beginning to honor them. Whatever mistakes they made, it's time for them to be forgiven as you have been forgiven. Write them down and hand judgment over to God.

2. *Write a Letter*

To your father, write a letter of all the things you respect about him. To your mother, write all of the things you love about her as a mother. This can be difficult, for some. Try to get someone with an outside perspective on your family to help if you end up hitting a wall here.

3. *Help Them*

If possible, find ways to help them. This can be money, time, or conversation. Especially as they age, treat your parents as you wish to be treated at that stage in your life. Again, not how they deserve, but how you wish to be treated.

4. *Pray for Them*

Begin regularly praying for your spiritual parents and those who raised you. If they are your enemies, pray for them even more.

Chapter 13

ENDURANCE

But the one who endures to the end will be saved.
—MATTHEW 24:13 ESV

Habit, as mundane and boring as that word may sound to you, is the thing that will separate you from those who try and eventually fail and those who endure. The simple, seemingly mundane habits of your daily life are the things that achieve great victory in the end.

Think of this in simple terms. When a man climbs Everest, what is he really doing? He is taking literally thousands of small steps; it is not done all at once. You do not simply appear at the top of a great peak. What someone is doing is not "climbing Everest." They are climbing, step by step, up a path laid before them to get to the top. The reality of the steps is different from the great achievement.

Most of your life is made up of simple decisions and simple habits. We acknowledge this easily in our minds but so rarely express it in our heart and actions.

It truly is the small things added together over time that transform your life. Far too many people are waiting for that big moment of transformation. The supernatural experience that will wash over them like magic fairy dust and make them the person (finally) God has *really* called them to be. It is true—these big moments do happen, but there is always a foundation of endurance.

In 2016, my wife and I moved to southern California to start a church. We were living in New York City before the move, as campus pastors in Manhattan. New York is the place where we fell in love, had our first child, and cut our teeth in ministry. New York had taught us how to endure. As newlyweds, we moved into a 650-square-foot apartment where the masonry dusted our faces as we slept, the bathroom door couldn't be opened at the same time as the refrigerator, and I could put my feet on the wall across from the couch as I watched TV. To us, though, it was our little newlywed paradise. I'll always have fond memories of that place where we got our start together. I walked in torn boots that got wet in the snow and rain, and we had knock-down drag-out fights about the budget when I said we couldn't eat out again this week.

Our campus was a raw group of young people who needed formation and direction, and we were in the thick of it in Manhattan. Despite all the difficulty, leadership failures, and the fight to build a Kingdom community in the midst of a pagan city, we had good times. Things got better financially as Jessi started a thriving business and I got a raise. We moved into a doorman building on the eleventh floor in lower Manhattan and everything was brand new.

I fasted and prayed at the beginning of 2016 as I was being given new responsibilities in the church, and we had our first little one, David, on the way. I was overwhelmed. In the midst of this time of prayer and fasting, God led my heart toward moving to California. We were soon talking it out with our lead pastors, which of course is not an easy conversation, for both sides, We weren't just a church family; my brother-in-law and sister were our leaders.

Add all of that stress together just when things seemed to be going quite well. We had money left over at the end of the month for the first time in our marriage. We had a baby on the way, I had full benefits and a stable and good ministry job on the main stage of ministry in the United States. It was a missionary type of job and we loved the fight. But God was telling us to move.

We packed everything into our miracle car (a Jeep Commander) and I drove across the country with my dad while my wife and mom flew to meet us there and move into an apartment sight unseen in Huntington Beach, California.

No back-up plan, a little bit of support, and a dream.

The time there was hard. Jessi was producing an income, I wasn't, and I pretended like I had work to do with a church of ten people. I went into a crisis while starting a church, while at the same time having grand visions of a house church network that would take over America. In the end, that is not what happened. The church failed—a thing impossible to not take personally. After four years of sowing into people, growing at one point to eight different house churches, it ended up all falling apart.

In the midst of this, all I had to hold on to in the dark of the morning was my secret place with Jesus, the confidence He placed in me and my calling, and my loving wife. I was learning to be a dad and seemingly alone. But I kept going. I kept being with Jesus. I kept my eyes focused on what God had placed in my heart.

My wife, Jessi, and I spent four years plowing the ground. Working hard. Inviting people into our home, and continuing to press on.

Our transformational moment and our call to California came in a way that I did not at all expect. Jessi had a vision of thousands being baptized in the ocean in California. In early 2020, God said to move forward with this vision. Gather people together, share the gospel, and baptize. As many of you reading this will recall, 2020 was not an ideal time to gather people out in the open. The overreaching Covid response hit California, and we thought this was our way out of doing what God had asked us to do. This was not the case.

So we met at Tower 20 in Huntington Beach the weekend of July 4, the same weekend the governor and many city councils shut down the beaches. Our social media was in an uproar as what came to be called "Saturate" took over the beach in California. We ended up being threatened with arrest, seeing vitriol and anger at what we were doing, and the vision came to pass in seeing thousands baptized on the beaches of California over a six-week period.

This was a transformational moment. But over eight years of ministry together we had pursued God, did the little things, and stuck to our family motto, "Obedience is success." We had a miraculous six weeks of acceleration, and it took eight years to get there.

Endurance means not always seeing the results you want. It means bearing the burden of your calling with grit and tenacity. It means when things look bleak, you cling to the one who saved you and called you. Endurance is always rewarded. This is a Christian virtue that has been so sidelined in my generation that I have alarming concerns about our ability to actually do the things we say we dream about. We have no grid for suffering and perseverance, and it shows.

Throw Out Your Microwave

We need to learn this again. We need to stop putting our lives in a microwave that creates cheap and tasteless meals. It is the difficulty in preparation that makes the victory so sweet. After all, why would a loving God give you something that would crush you?

"First prepare the field, and then build your house."

Make sure before you build the thing everyone can see that you have put in the ground what *nobody* can see. So that when your house is built, you have a place to put the harvest that you have sown in past seasons. Too many of us expect a harvest when we have put nothing in the ground to die.

In the end, this is what endurance really looks like. It looks like a continual dying of self so that the "self" that is raised in Christ Jesus can firmly take root and produce fruit. What good is a successful ministry without Jesus being your life? What good is a thriving business without people to bless with it? What good is a man if he gains the whole world yet loses his own soul?

We can be successful, but we must be careful not to equate God's version of success with the one that we have already created in our own minds. To endure is success. To be obedient is success. To die to yourself is success. To cling to Christ until the end of your days is success.

This is what this entire book has been about—the little things that really are, after all, the big things.

How can you practice endurance? How can you prepare yourself for all that life will throw at you in your marriage, your family, your ministry, your vocation, and all the other twists and turns that place you in situations that you've never dreamed of?

It is something that too many know and far too few practice. It is the daily, ruthless, endless, pursuit of Jesus. You know exactly what you need to do. What makes the difference in the end is whether or not you actually do it.

It is time for a generation to learn to endure for Christ. And having done all, to stand.

Don't quit, for the time is short and the days are dark. You are the city set on a hill. For your own sake and the sake of the generations to come, endure.

The Path

How can a person build endurance into their daily life? I'll put a few steps in here that I have done over time that have given me more ability to simply endure through difficult seasons and accept the good ones. What we are aiming to build is enduring faith, despite our circumstances.

Here, I want you to write down in your journal exactly *why* you follow Jesus. Then write down what you do in order to follow Him. A deep conviction and vision for your life from God will give you the ability to pursue discipline. Many try to do it the other way around, but that's not how we operate. Human beings need to know, or at least feel, why they are doing something.

Go ahead and write it down. If you're having a hard time knowing why exactly you follow Jesus, start with how you got saved by Him.

About Parker Green

Parker Green is a husband, father of three, preacher, and co-founder of Saturate Global, The Commission Training Center, and Salt Church. He lives and breathes to see people meet Jesus and follow Him with every detail of their lives. His core message is that spiritual discipline is the doorway to a life fully alive in Christ and a deep response to His saving grace. His greatest joy in life is to be a husband, a father to his children, and to teach the way of Jesus that leads to the Father, the Giver of all things. Also, it must be mentioned he is a slightly above average cross-fitter and Land Cruiser driver.